Cyril Joe Barton V.C.

by
W.W. Lowther

WEAR BOOKS

© Wear Books 1994
First published 1994

Wear Books, Central Library, Borough Road, Sunderland, SR1 1PP

ISBN 0 905108 39 6

Printed by Printcentre, Roker Baths Road, Sunderland

Contents

Introduction		5
Acknowledgements		5
Chapters		
1.	The Formative Years, 1921–41	6
2.	The Making of a Bomber Pilot	11
3.	The Raid on Nuremberg	24
4.	The View from Ryhope	35
5.	Aftermath—New Malden	48
6.	Epilogue	54
Appendices		
Appendix I	The Cyril Barton Memorial Campaign	55
II	P/O Cyril Barton V.C. Memorial List	61
III	Victor 'Raid on Nuremberg'	63
Bibliography		65

Foreword

My research into the life of Cyril Barton came about as a direct result of a proposal by Sunderland Leisure, Libraries and Arts Section, who felt that such a study would be most appropriate, as 1994 marks the fiftieth anniversary of the pilot's posthumous award of the Victoria Cross following his heroic actions during the ill-fated Nuremberg raid, which culminated in his tragic crash-landing in the north-eastern village of Ryhope.

A local history enthusiast, Alan Kinsley, volunteered his assistance, as did Elaine Naylor, Community Librarian for Ryhope. Our progress was greatly expedited by the 'recruitment' of Alan Mitcheson with his veritable storehouse of source materials relating to Cyril Barton.

We have pieced together the albeit brief life of this extraordinary individual from a range of eyewitness accounts, photographs, official documents and contemporary letters and, as far as possible, we have allowed the sources to speak for themselves.

Bill Lowther
March, 1994

Acknowledgements

We are indebted to some very kind people who were willing not only to be interviewed, but to lend much treasured photographs, letters and other memorabilia. They are: Joyce Voysey, Cynthia Maidment, Len Lambert, Ken and Tom Richardson, Arthur Milburn and Les Lawther.

Our thanks also go to the Department of Research and Information Services, RAF Museum, Hendon, and Jack Hedley at Ryhope Community Centre. Typing skills were provided by Chris Weston, Brenda Dick and Jude Letham, while Bob Watt gave invaluable cartographic assistance. Grammatical errors were painstakingly corrected by Robin Stewart and Paula McNeany. Crucial financial support came from Sunderland Leisure, Libraries and Arts, and Wearside College.

For these, and for permission to use extracts from 'Raider', written by Geoffrey Jones and published by Harper Collins, and to the Ordnance Survey, we are most grateful.

Bill Lowther
Alan Mitcheson
Alan Kinsley
Elaine Naylor
Mary Dobson

Chapter 1
The Formative Years, 1921–1941

The Barton Family c.1940. Back Row left to right: Mr. & Mrs. Barton, Roy, Ken, George (cousin), Cyril. Front Row left to right: Pam, Cynthia & Joyce.

Cyril Barton was born on June 5th, 1921 at Elvedon in Suffolk, the eldest of a family of six children. Soon after his birth, his family left Suffolk for Surrey. His father, Frederick, was an electrical engineer who worked on large landed estates so the family usually lived in tithe cottages. His sisters remember their early years:

Cynthia:

"During the 1930's, Dad was earning about £3 a week; 19 shillings (95p) went on rent; the rest of the money went on paying bills and buying food for the eight of us. Mum managed but there was no money left for treats . . . however, we never lacked for love and affection. Cyril and Ken were both resourceful. If they needed toys, they made them.

When I was five, they went down to the local rubbish dump. They found a boy's bicycle frame with some wheels and so they built my first bicycle and painted it blue with Minnie Mouses on it.

Joyce:

"We had a metal bed and they painted that blue as well."

Cynthia:

"Usually, by the time Dad returned at night,

Roy, Ken and Cyril with the 'Shell Tanker' c.1932.

c.1938   Back row: Ken, Mum, Pam, Cyril.
Front row: Joyce, Roy and Cynthia.

we would be in bed so Cyril was like a little father to us."

Cynthia:

"He always had time to show us girls what to do . . . we would learn from him how to do things . . . even things which were considered in those days to be women's jobs . . . he taught us to sew, and to knit, and to draw."

Joyce:

"He always remembered other people and never forgot a birthday. Even when he was seriously ill in hospital, he recorded in his diary on March 3rd, 'I don't know what to get Dad for his birthday'.

His priority was other people all the time. Among Cyril's possessions sent to us after his death was a birthday card for me."

Cynthia:

"He was so full of fun. I remember when I was five years old, Cyril gave me a penny to take to the sweet shop and he told me to ask for a pennyworth of shillings. When Roy and I came out of the shop, Cyril and Ken were in hysterics.

He was always interested in aeroplanes. I remember a plane came overhead and crash landed in a roof nearby. Cyril and Ken rushed me in a pushchair to the scene of the crash."

Joyce:

"That was 1937. Cyril, who was 16, recorded in his diary, 'Hard Luck, I didn't get any souvenirs'."

Joyce:

"Cyril was bright but his school reports do not recognise this. His education was affected by a number of serious illnesses. He was thirteen when he was first poorly and developed meningitis so that's when he missed a lot of schooling. When he was about fifteen – he must have been at technical college – he was taken ill with peritonitis. He was in hospital for nearly three months. The police came twice for Mum and Dad to see him for the last time. They said that he just wouldn't pull through. But Mum said after she went to see him that last time, 'He is going to pull through. I won't let anything happen to him.' He was supposed to be careful about what he ate . . . Mum

". . . always interested in aeroplanes." c.1935.

CYRIL BARTON V.C.

SURREY EDUCATION COMMITTEE.

(Stamp: NEW MALDEN BEVERLEY CENTRAL SCHOOL)

_____ Central School.

Report for Term ended **31 JUL 1935**

Name: Cyril Barton Age: 14 ½ yr.

Form: IV Average Age of Form: 14 ½ yr.

Subject.	Exam. Mark.		Term's Work.	Remarks.
Scripture			F.G.	
English: Language & Literature	70	29	F.	Some improvement evident:
Reading & Recitation	30	21	F.G.	should aim at being more
Essay & Correspondence	100	72	G.	uniform.
History	F		F.	Hardly satisfactory
Geography			F. Good	
Mathematics:	100	60	G.	Great improvement. More settled this term
French				
Science			F Good.	Is improving.
Domestic Subjects				
Needlework				
Handicraft				
Gardening				
Drawing (Geometry)				
Drawing:			F.G.	Satisfactory
Book-Keeping				
Shorthand				
Homework				

Total Marks obtained	182	Position in Form	8th.	Times Absent	5
" " possible	300	Number "	20	" Late	0

General Remarks— Conduct V. Good.

Improvement shown — a fairly good term's work.

H.B. Umpelby, Form Teacher.

W G Heal, Head Teacher.

took him up anything he wanted. She had made up her mind he was going to get better."

Joyce:
"Cyril recorded in his diary, 'Mum came up today . . . Mum brought me a glider to make.' (Every day Mrs. Barton visited Cyril despite having five other children to look after, the youngest of whom was only twelve months old).

She made up her mind that he was going to get better, and he did, but it took a long time – three months in hospital – and then he went to convalesce. After that he went to Yorkshire to stay with relatives. By that time he was sixteen."[1]

Cyril Barton and Religion

The Reverend Frank Colquhoun M.A, St. John's Church, New Malden, c 1937-41:
"I first met Cyril when he was about to leave school. From this point also dates the beginning of his radiant Christian experience.

Some people have asked me about Cyril's conversion – how he became a Christian. I do not know that there is actually very much to be said about that. There was certainly nothing sensational or spectacular about his decision for Christ. His Bible class . . . was, I know, a big factor in his spiritual life. His attendance of the class was most regular and he showed his keenness not only by coming himself but by bringing other boys with him."[2]

Maurice Divey, a friend of Cyril, recalls:
"We were active members of the church and together with a handful of teenagers ran, amongst other things, the Youth Club. He was a very committed Christian and often led our discussion groups at the club. But he was full of fun and enjoyed life immensely. One night, he turned up on his old bike which he had very carefully painted a gleaming black and, along the side of the front mudguard, he had painted in white the word 'ICHABOD'. We pulled his leg a bit over this and asked him why he had called his bike ICHABOD. 'Well,' he said, with a twinkle in his eye, 'if you lot care to look at the Old Testament you'll find it's a Hebrew name meaning 'No Glory' – well that's my bike!'"[3]

'Ichabod', 'No glory – that's my bike!' c.1938.

Cynthia:
"We were brought up in a very happy loving atmosphere and that was how Christianity was brought across to us . . . mainly through Cyril and Ken. Cyril never rammed his beliefs down anyone's throat. He lived what he felt. He had a great aura . . . Everyone, not just brothers and sisters, was drawn to him. His affection, his smile, his influence—he was always happy and inspired those around him."[4]

After School

Joyce:
On leaving school, he went to work for

Parnell's, the local aircraft factory. A gentleman there saw what ability he had and persuaded my parents to put him in for an apprenticeship as a draughtsman.

Shortly after the war began, in 1939, we moved to be away from the raids (1940). We went up to Suffolk, first of all to Newmarket where my father worked for twelve months and then we went on to Great Barton near Bury St. Edmunds, but Cyril stayed behind and lived with his Bible class leader, Mr. Juden in Surbiton, Surrey."[5]

This was during the winter of 1940-1941 when the blitz was at its height. It was during this experience of continuous raiding that they both decided to join the RAF. They discussed the situation together and reached the conclusion that unless the power of Nazi Germany was broken, the whole world would be in danger of being submerged by the Antichrist . . .

It had always been Cyril's ambition to fly and now his opportunity had come. He would offer himself to train as a pilot.[6]

Cyril needed his father's permission before he could volunteer for the RAF. His father, who had experienced the horrors of trench warfare during the First World War, was somewhat less enthusiastic about his son's request.

Letter to Cyril from his father c.1941:

"Dear Cyril,

After all these letters . . . and phone calls and so on, I have weighed up your position and feel that the matter should rest entirely with you. Naturally your Mother and I are not too keen on your 'joining up', more especially as I know by experience what such a step entails, but in view of what you have said regarding your present stay with Parnell's, I rather grudgingly give my consent.

I rang your firm and . . . they said they could get your exemption and were surprised to think that you had found it necessary to leave them . . . They were quite confident that they could exempt you on the strength of your medical record and would do their utmost to this end.

. . . I am writing as requested, to both the Air Ministry and Parnell's, and in doing so I wish you every success and a happy ending to your enthusiasm. Stick to your principles and have faith . . .

. . . I'll close now and may God bless you and help you in the days that lie ahead.

That is my greatest wish and hope . . . Goodbye and 'Happy Landings'.

Dad"

References

[1] *Interview with Barton's sisters Cynthia Maidment and Joyce Voysey, 27th November, 1993*
[2] *Frank Colquhoun M.A. 'The Air Pilot's Decision', Guildford, reprinted 1982, pp. 7-8*
[3] *Maurice Divey's letter dated 28th September, 1993*
[4] *Interview with Cynthia Maidment*
[5] *Interview with Joyce Voysey*
[6] *F. Colquhoun: 'The Air Pilot's Decision', p.11, pp. 15-18*

Chapter 2

The Making of a Bomber Pilot

First successful solo flight completed 19th Feb, 1942.

Cyril Barton joined the RAF on 16th April, 1941 and, on completion of his basic training, was promoted to Leading Aircraftsman on 1st November. The USA's entry into the war, in December, 1941 opened the way for Cyril and many of his contemporaries to learn the art of flying in the New World.

On 19th January, 1942, he made his first supervised flight in a PT 17 trainer at Darr Aero Technical School, Albany, Georgia.[1]

From 4th to 7th September, 1942, he continued his training at Cochran Field, Macon, flying BT13A's. This was followed by advanced training in the more powerful AT6 aircraft at Napier Field, Duthan, Alabama, from which Sergeant Barton graduated on 10th November, 1942.

Cyril and Doreen

On his return to England, Cyril spent much of January and February, 1943 in Harrogate, Yorkshire and it was here that he met Doreen. He described the meeting in a letter to his brother, Ken:

> Majestic Hotel,
> Harrogate
>
> Jan 1943

"Dear Ken,

. . . I guess you'll be surprised and perhaps amused to hear I've got a girlfriend here.

I met her two weeks ago at a Methodist church servicemen's club . . . They serve suppers at this place for 4d, which isn't bad going. You get quite a few cakes and as many cups of tea as you like for that price. On top of this, it is served to you at your table as if you were at a café. The young lady who brought mine to me started off a conversation by remarking that I was a stranger here. After a while . . . well, we found that we were both 'crusaders' in the wider meaning of the word.

She later introduced me to her father who was also helping there, and whom I had previously given a game of billiards, without knowing who he was.

They invited me to their house after the evening service on Sunday . . . Well after that I went to their house several times. The girl's name is Doreen W_____ and we have been out together several times since. Well, now you've read all this I can see your face split from ear to ear in a tremendous grin – that's how it strikes me too. If you had told me a fortnight ago that I should even have spoken to a girl in Harrogate, I would have

Barton's Flight Log February–May, 1942

Year 1942 Month/Date	Aircraft Type	No.	Pilot, or 1st Pilot	2nd Pilot, Pupil or Passenger	Duty (Including Results and Remarks)	Single-Engine Day Dual	Single-Engine Day Pilot
					Totals Brought Forward	11:49	1:03
Feb. 12	PT.17		Seimer C.R.	Self	Landings & take offs, pattern entry.	0:44	
Feb. 14	"			Self	Third supervised solo. Three circuits on home field.		0:28
" 15	"		Seimer C.R.	Self	Stalls, spins, steep & med. turns, elementary eights. "S" turns simulated forced landing. Revision of work.	0:53	
" 18	"		"	"	Stalls, spins, steep turns, elementary eights, coordination exercises, chandelles, simulated forced landing.	0:50	
" 19	"	24	Self		First unsupervised solo. Stalls, spins, co ordination exercises. Landing & take off.		1:05
" 20	"		Seimer C.R.	Self	Spins, stalls, steep turns, chandelles, elementary eights, "S" turns	0:40	
				Grand Total 17 Hrs 32 Mins	Totals Carried Forward	14:56	2:36

Year 1942 Month/Date	Aircraft Type	No.	Pilot, or 1st Pilot	2nd Pilot, Pupil or Passenger	Duty (Including Results and Remarks)	Dual	Pilot
					Totals Brought Forward	14:56	2:36
Feb. 20	PT.17		Self		Stalls, spins, steep turns, chandelles, elementary eights.		1:21
" 21	"	39	"		Stalls, spins with precision recovery, steep turns, chandelles.		0:58
" 22	"		Seimer C.R.	Self	Stalls, spins, chandelles.	1:11	
May 16	"		Minske D.H.	"	Revision of work.	0:35	
" 18	"		"	"	Landings & take offs.	0:15	
" 18	"		Self	"	Landings & take offs.		0:10
" 19	"		Minske D.H.	Self	Landings & take offs.	0:15	
" 19	"		Self		Landings & take-offs.		0:32
" 20	"	10	"		Stalls, spins, chandelles, elementary eights		0:45
" 21	"		Minske D.H.	Self	Stalls, spins, chandelles, elementary eights.	0:45	
				Grand Total 24 Hrs 19 Mins	Totals Carried Forward	17:57	6:22

Barton's Flight Log February–May, 1942

called you a liar. No doubt about it, it IS darned funny!

I would be less surprised if YOU found a girl, but ME, well it beats me! However, until I met her I had no Christian friend here and it has meant a lot to me in this respect alone . . ."

Cyril and Doreen, 1943.

A relaxed Sgt. Barton visits his mother in Surbiton, Surrey, 1943.

Despite his good fortune, Cyril could not hide his dissatisfaction with the local RAF administration.

"A few days ago we loaded up with two full kitbags and webbing and wandered across to the 'Grand Hotel', looking like a lot of pack mules. After taking the trouble to inform a lot of people the change of address, we moved back to 'The Majestic' again, today."

Flight Sergeant Barton, September 1943.

On arrival in Kinloss, Sgt. Barton's main task was to find and train a bomber crew.

On 15th March, 1943, he was posted to No 6 AFU (Advanced Flying Unit), Chipping Norton, before joining No. 19 OTU (Operational Training Unit), Kinloss, Morayshire on 4th May, 1943.[3]

Barton's crew

Len Lambert:

"We went to a big house near the airfield, one of those country houses which the Air Force took over and they laid on tea and coffee and things and tried to make it a social thing, rather like going to a dance and being switched round to meet the girls, but here you were just encouraged to walk around and chat with other members because they were all like me, newly qualified, newly got their wings and that's how I met Cyril Barton. We got talking and must have had something in common and Cyril Barton said, 'Would you like to be my Navigator?' and I said, 'Yes if you will put up with me,' and that's how we got started. From there he invited Jack Kay to be our wireless operator and Freddie Brice, the rear gunner and Wally Crate – he was the Canadian bomb-aimer. The four of us came together on that coffee morning, we got talking to each other and came out of it as a crew. We were very lucky, we were a good crew and got on well together. So that is how I first met him and we did quite a lot of flying from May to June. Everything happened so quickly, two months there and, by the time we finished that course, we went on to the Heavy Conversion Unit at Rufforth near York where we converted from Whitleys to the four-engined Halifax Bomber. We added two other members of the crew, the Flight Engineer, which a four-engined bomber required and that happened to be a local man from Heaton in Newcastle, Maurice Trousdale, and also Harry 'Timber' Wood. We all got on well together as a crew."[4]

Freddie Brice:

"From the start we all got along fine so I guess

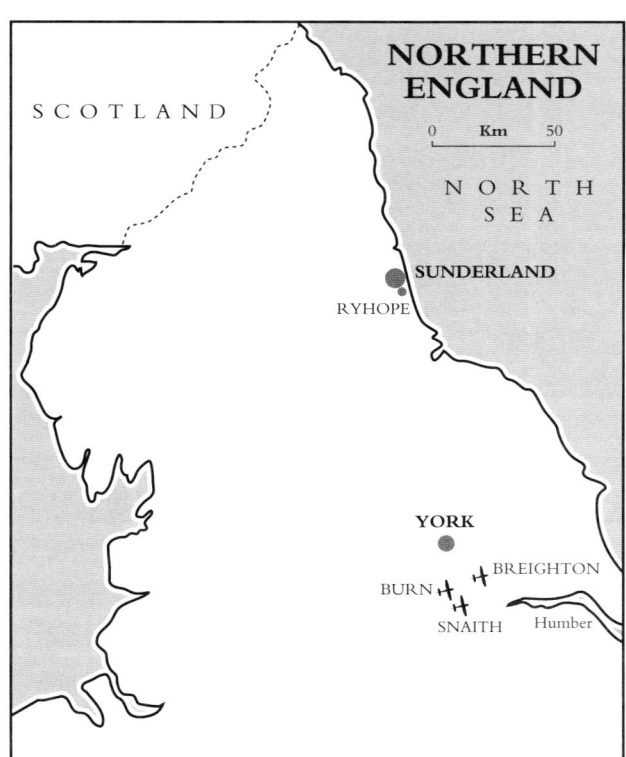

CYRIL BARTON V.C.

CERTIFICATES OF QUALIFICATION AS FIRST PILOT

R.C.A.F. Form R.95
(R.A.F. 414)
20M-12-41 (1371)
H.Q. 1062-3-78

Name *Barton CJ 168669* Rank *Sgt*

(i) Certified that the above named has qualified as a first pilot (day) ~~night~~ on *Whitley L* landplanes w.e.f. *1st July 1943*
Unit *19 O.T.U.* Signature
Date *3rd July 1943* Rank

Barton's Certificate of qualification as a pilot

First crew photograph with 78 Squadron at Breighton, 1943. Standing left to right: Sgt. Kay, P/O Crate, P/O Barton, Sgt. Lambert, Sgt. Trousdale; front left to right: Sgt. Brice, Sgt. Wood.

Cyril was a fine judge of men."[5]

Qualities of leadership

Freddie Brice:

"I had little fear flying with him, never any panic and his whole calmness seemed to reach us all."[6]

Len Lambert:

"Cyril Barton was a very confident pilot and he had a nice way with him. He was strict in his ideas as to how things should be done but he had a nice easy-going way of putting it over. For example, he wouldn't allow any swearing while we were flying and we always had to use the absolute minimum of words when we were speaking over the intercom in the aircraft; it had to be pilot to navigator, navigator to pilot: what we had to say, no chatter or anything else when we were flying: we had to concentrate on what we were doing.

There was a lot of hard work to do; our lives depended on knowing what we had to do, and really, we were trained to be pilots in a relatively short time. Some people perhaps could stand up to it better than others but there was a fair amount of stress about and we were growing up too and the girlfriends were always in the background there."[7]

Operational service

As well as working with his new team, Cyril Barton was assigned as second pilot to experienced bomber crews. On 24th and 27th July he took part in his first raids – target: Hamburg.[8]

Six days before the first of these 'ops', Sergeant Barton had written a letter which he deposited with his brother, Ken, with instructions to forward it to his mother in the event of the pilot's death.

RAF Rufforth

18th July '43

"Dear Mum,

I hope you never receive this but I quite expect you will. I'm expecting to do my first operational trip in a few days. I know what ops over Germany means and I have no illusions about it. By my own calculations the average life of a crew is 20 ops and we have thirty to do in our first 'tour'.

I'm writing this for two reasons. One to tell you how I would like my money spent that I have left behind; two, to tell you how I feel about meeting my Maker.

1. I intended, as you know, taking a university course with my savings. Well, I would like it to be spent on the education of my brothers and sisters. Ken is a bit old to start part-time study now and I would like him to have as much of it as he needs for full-time study, all of it if he can use it. Roy is still young and has his 'teens before him, it's up to him to help himself. The girls likewise. I'll leave it to you to decide what to do with my belongings.

2. All I can say about this is that I'm quite prepared to die, it holds no terror for me. I know I shall survive the judgement because I have trusted in Christ as my own Saviour, I've done nothing to merit glory, but because He died for me it's God's free gift. At times I've wondered whether I've been right believing what I do and just recently I've doubted the veracity of the Bible, but in the little time I've had to sort out intellectual problems I've been left with a bias in favour of the Bible. Apart from this I have the inner conviction as I write, a force outside myself and my brain, that I have not trusted in vain. All I am anxious about is that you and the rest of the family will also come to know Him. Ken, I know, already does. I commend my Saviour to you.

I am writing to Doreen separately. I expect you will have guessed by now that we are quite in love with each other. She, too, will find the

Flight Sergeant Barton leads his untested crew into action—15th September—target: Montlucon

blow hard to bear but there is a text we have often quoted to each other and is written in the 'Daily Light' she gave me – Romans 8.28. It's true.

Well, that's covered everything now I guess, so,

Love to Dad and all,
Your loving son,
Cyril."

The conversion training on Halifax bombers was completed by the end of August 1943 when Barton and his crew were transferred to Breighton airfield, where they joined their operational unit, 78 Squadron. At the same time, 5th September, Cyril Barton was promoted to Flight Sergeant.[9]

"The tension was very high the first time we went out, but it was a very easy raid, the only one we didn't go to Germany. We raided a place called Montlucon in France. There was a big tyre factory there, a big industrial complex. It was very easy the first trip, I think that helped because it was surprising the number of people that didn't return from their first trip and your confidence built up from that."[10]

By the end of September, 1943, the fledgling crew had carried out a further four raids, against Hanover (twice), Mannheim and Bochum. The harsh realities of life in Bomber Command, however, were soon to become apparent.

Len Lambert:

"I was wounded in November, 1943 on our sixth raid. This was a raid on Leverkusen, an industrial town on the Rhine, a big chemical

Year 1943		Aircraft		Pilot, or 1st Pilot	2nd Pilot, Pupil or Passenger	Duty (Including Results and Remarks)	Multi-Engine Aircraft Day 1st Pilot (6)	2nd Pilot (7)	Dual (8)	Night 1st Pilot (9)	2nd Pilot (10)
Month	Date	Type	No.								
						Totals Brought Forward	81:25	40:20	14:25	87:50	29:45
Oct.	13	Halifax	Z	Lt. Kelly, Self	Sgts. Bryce Stainer, Wood	Fighter Affiliation	:30	:30			
Oct.	27	Link	—	—	—	I/F Revision					
Nov.	5	Halifax	Z	Self	Crew F/Lt. Hammond	Air Test					
Nov.	19	Halifax	W	Self	Crew Sgt. Melville (2nd Pilot)	Ops Leverkusen. Navigator & Air bomber injured by flak. Landed Woodbridge.				4:50	
Nov.	22/23	Halifax	J	Self	Crew	Ops. Berlin.				7:15	
Nov.	23	Halifax	Z	Self	Crew	Air Test.	:25				
Nov.	25	Halifax	Z	Self	Crew	Ops. Frankfort.				7:20	
Nov.	25/26	Halifax	Z	Self	Crew	Ops. Stuttgart. Landed Leconfield.				8:15	
Nov.	28	Halifax	Z	Self	Sgts. Kay & Trousdale	Return. Leconfield to base.	:20				
Summary for Oct. & Nov. Unit 78 Sqn. Date 30th Nov. 43 Signature Cyril J Barton, A/Sgt.					Aircraft Types.	Halifax	2:15	:30		30:50	

Year 1943		Aircraft		Pilot, or 1st Pilot	2nd Pilot, Pupil or Passenger	Duty (Including Results and Remarks)	Multi-Engine Aircraft Day 1st Pilot (6)	2nd Pilot (7)	Dual (8)	Night 1st Pilot (9)	2nd Pilot (10)
Month	Date	Type	No.								
						Totals Brought Forward	83:40	40:50	14:25	118:20	29:45
Dec.	5	Link		Self	—	S.B.A. & I/F Practice					
"	18	"		"		35 Sqn. method S.B.A. circuit					
"	19	"		"		"					
"	29	Halifax	W	Self	Crew	Fighter Afaliation	1:10				
"	29	"	W	"	"	Ops. Berlin. Landed Grimsby.				8:35	
"	30	"	W	"	"	Grimsby to Base.	0:25				
"	31	Link		"		Timed circuit (SBA)					
Summary for Dec. '43 78 Sqn. 31st Dec. '43 Cyril J Barton, A/Sgt.						Halifax Link	1:35			8:35	
				Grand Total [Cols. (1) to (10)] 559 Hrs. 00 Mins.		Totals Carried Forward	85:15	40:50	14:25	126:55	29:45

Operations November–December, 1943

With twelve raids to his credit, the ever-smiling Cyril Barton was promoted to Pilot Officer on January 5th 1944.

complex rather like ICI at Billingham. There was pretty serious flak damage to most of the aircraft. I got a piece that came up through the floor that fractured my skull and I was off two months with that. The bomb-aimer also got a piece through his leg and that kept him out of action for a while. Cyril Barton was the pilot and we managed to make an emergency landing at Woodbridge, near Ipswich, a big airfield on the coast If you had anything wrong, you could fly in there and they had all the facilities. I managed to navigate. It was one of those things that looked worse than it was. There was blood all over the place – you know what it is if you cut anything. I got a fractured skull and a bit of bone was taken and grafted and the hole filled in. I don't know what I would have been like without it. I seem to have coped all right but, anyway, it did take two months to get over and therefore I missed a number of flights with the crew, from November 19th. It wasn't until January 28th that I flew with them again."[11]

On January 15, 1944, Barton and his crew were

Halifax Mk. III: this was the only type of aircraft to be flown by 578 Squadron.

posted to Snaith airfield where a new squadron, 578, was formed from 'C' Flight. Having flown operations in Halifax Mk II's, the crew were now converted to the Halifax Mk III.

On the night of 30th January, Cyril Barton completed his third trip to Berlin and, the following week, 578 Squadron moved from Snaith to Burn airfield. [12]

Handling the pressure

Len Lambert:

"Growing confidence among the crew didn't mean there wasn't stress. It was true to say that I can't imagine any members of aircrew Bomber Command suffering from constipation!

I myself became very detached. You imagine things happening to other people and not you. You really didn't have time to make friends; you go to these reunions and you are just recounting your experiences at that time, but very seldom do you come across people who you actually knew. You would hear of a crew going missing and you probably only vaguely remember what they looked like. I think that probably made it easier but, nevertheless, we were fully aware of the risks but I don't think we talked about it very much. It just made us think very hard as to how keen and efficient we had to be to have a chance of survival, do everything very quickly and not to have any idle chatter when we were actually flying. But you really had a tightening of the tummy muscles, the colly-wobbles on your way out to the aircraft. Once you got in and sat down to your job, you didn't feel it at all. The navigator was working hard all the time; other crew members would feel sorry for the rear gunner because he just had to sit there and watch out into the darkness for hour after hour and then have to suddenly jerk into action.

After I was wounded, I wondered if I was good enough for the crew to get us back every time. But I got us back when I was wounded. I seem to remember worrying not so much as to whether I would survive myself, but as to whether I was good enough to get the crew as a whole to survive because it's a nasty feeling getting lost in the air. A lot of people lost their lives because their navigators got lost.

People have the idea that all the lads in the Air Force were heavy drinkers during the war and a bit wild but we were just really overgrown schoolboys. I don't think I really touched alcohol when I was in the Air Force. We used to go to the NAAFI for a cup of tea, while some of the crew members did go to the pub to drink. Cyril Barton and I didn't. I never found the need for it, the same way as I never smoked and a lot of people smoked then, but I think probably about half the crew drank and smoked, possibly less than half.

Cyril was very open-minded. He was a deeply religious person but really we didn't find that out until afterwards. When I say we didn't find out, we knew he went to church but that wasn't so unusual; I was a keen churchgoer. I was brought up as a Methodist; he was an Anglican. He accepted other people's points of view and he would often go out with the lads to the pub and buy them a round of drinks, perhaps just have a lemonade himself, or he would buy a round of drinks and then go with me to the pictures because I was straight from school and pubs really weren't my scene.

We went around as a crew quite often. I remember going to Leeds, the whole lot of us, and going to a café in one of the department stores there. We were having our meal and a lady at a table nearby just came and gave us all twenty Players. Half of us didn't smoke, we didn't know how to, but people were very good. We had some escapades. The Canadian bomb aimer was a lovely bloke, very soft-spoken and not a bit wild, but I remember we got off a train, it was late, and he said we are not going to bother going through the barrier. We just leaped over the fence and of course we were collared by the RAF police on the other side. They were only doing their job.

The Barton crew's 'Observation' book

We had some fun. It is difficult to remember everything we did. We got round to each other's homes. Certainly all the crew visited my parents in Newcastle when Wally Crate and I were in hospital after being wounded. The whole crew came back there to see us.

While I was at Burn, we got very close together, Cyril Barton and I and the rest of the crew too. We went to the little local Methodist church and we were befriended by the Websters who had a farm there. They used to invite us over for supper on a Sunday after church and it was they who christened us 'Barton's Barmy Bomber Boys', and Mrs. Webster would make these big apple pies. She had the pastry cut out 'BBBB'. The Websters were always at the end of the runway to wave us off when we went away."[13]

Cyril Barton's faith and his work as a bomber pilot

Early in 1944, when Cynthia was twelve years old, Cyril came home on leave.

Cynthia:

"I was upset and jealous because he had a young lady friend . . . He tried to explain to me what the war was all about . . . and how he felt about having to kill . . . He didn't like it . . . but he explained how Hitler was trying to rule the world and bring about a special breed of people, which he thought was wrong. Although he did not like doing what he was doing, he felt it had to be done for the safety of his family. He also knew that there were times when his bombs must have killed other people's children and that used to upset him . . . He found that aspect very difficult to cope with . . . I do remember him being very upset about that."

Cynthia detected a change in him after he had started bombing operations over Nazi-occupied Europe.

"He was much more serious but he would always make a big effort to be his old self in front of us. Whenever he came home, there was always fun, I remember the last time he came home: he went straight down to the shed, made a sledge and took us girls out on it . . . but he was a lot more serious. I remember Mum and Dad saying how he had grown up in that time and obviously it used to devastate them. But we didn't actually see him many times during the war."[14]

As well as facing up to his service responsibilities, Cyril Barton also conducted a secret inner struggle. Two weeks before the fateful raid on Nuremberg, he confessed to a Christian friend:

"After I left you on Monday I had a whole lot to think about. During the rest of our leave I decided that when I went back to camp I would openly kneel in my bed in prayer every night – something I have funked since my first days in the RAF. As perhaps I told you, I share a room with Wally my bomb aimer, and Jack my wireless operator, the only other two officers in the crew. They know what I believe to a certain extent, and take care not to offend me. However, I felt that my witness was not as vigorous as it should be, and I knew that if I did not do anything about it, I would only slip back – and if I did, it would cost me a lot. I could not face the one any more than the other; but I think that the Lord made up my mind for me.

I was still undecided on Friday evening when I met Doreen at the station in Harrogate. Just before the train went I asked her to pray that the Lord would give me strength when I got back to camp to do something that I had failed to do since I joined up, but did not say what. She promised – and kept it.

After that I could not go back on it; but I was rather disappointed when neither Wally nor Jack were back when I arrived. Next day Wally and I were in the billet together and when I went to bed Wally was busy writing; but although I was on my knees for about ten minutes I'm sure he did not even notice me.

The third night I went to the local Methodist church with all the crew except Wally and Jack. When I got back they were sound asleep! You don't know how much it took out of me, being the third night in succession that the opportunity had been taken away. However, last night I was on my knees and in prayer when Wally came in. I've been in some tight corners over Germany (and I am not shooting a line, I really have!) but my heart never dropped with such a bump as when that door opened! I have never felt so lonely in my life. Wally made no comment that I could hear, but tip-toed around the room until I got up.

When I did so I was in a cold sweat, but Wally broke into conversation as if nothing had happened . . . I'd like to ask you to pray on that I may find His grace to see this thing through."

On March 28, 1944 he declared his personal victory:

"Nine days after I came back from leave I got the opportunity that I had been waiting for. I had been to church and when I got back Jack and Wally were in and listening to the radio. It was fairly late so I got undressed and excused myself from conversation by saying that I was off the 'intercom' for ten minutes, and knelt by my bed. Jack very reverently turned down his favourite radio programme and an awkward hush settled on the room. The Lord was very real to me for a few minutes and I was very thankful to Him for bringing me through, whatever the consequences might be.

When I got up they both tried to carry on as though nothing had happened, and made no comment. However, Jack was so badly shaken that he left his radio on (just humming) until after he had got into bed and would have forgotten altogether if I had not reminded him that it was on . . . It still seems difficult to believe that something I had almost given up as hopeless has actually been achieved after three years."

The letter ended on an equally optimistic note:

"I have now done eighteen ops and am looking forward to finishing within a reasonably short time."[15]

References

[1] *Cyril Barton's Flight Log Book*
[2] *Ibid.*
[3] *Ibid.*
[4] *Interview with Len Lambert, 7th November, 1993*
[5] *Letter from F. Brice to A. Mitcheson, 28th May, 1982*
[6] *Ibid.*
[7] *Interview with Len Lambert, 7th November, 1993*
[8] *Cyril Barton's Flight Log Book*
[9] *Ibid.*
[10] *Interview with Len Lambert, 7th November, 1993*
[11] *Ibid.*
[12] *Cyril Barton's Flight Log Book*
[13] *Interview with Len Lambert 7th November, 1993*
[14] *Interview with Cynthia Maidment*
[15] *Frank Colquhoun: 'The Air Pilot's Decision'*

Chapter 3

The Raid on Nuremberg

March, 1944 started badly for Cyril Barton. On the first day of the month, the brakes on his Halifax III had proved to be unserviceable with the result that the bomber ran off the end of the runway on landing. During a raid on Stuttgart on the night of 16th/17th March, his new aircraft, LK797 'E', developed problems with the oxygen supply to the mid-upper turret whilst flying over the target area. Two nights later, the bomb doors failed to open over Frankfurt. The bombs were eventually jettisoned over Darmstadt and LK797 'E' had to land at Burn with the bomb doors still open. However, these teething problems were overcome and, between 22nd and 26th March, Barton's Bomber Boys and LK797 'E' carried out successful operations over Frankfurt, Berlin and Essen.[1]

"While executing the last of these raids, Cyril Barton was unaware that his promotion to Flying Officer had been decided by the powers that be.

As confidence in their new bomber developed, Barton's crew decided on a suitable emblem which was then chalked onto the nose of the Halifax. This emblem featured the sword 'Excalibur' striking down from the clouds towards a burning swastika. Before painting their creation however, the crew had to prepare for their next operational flight. It was to be 'Cy' Barton's 19th raid - and his last."[2]

The raid on Nuremberg, March 30th/31st, 1944, was to be one of the last shows of strength by Bomber Command over Germany before concentrating its efforts upon preparations for D-Day. Accordingly, 795 Lancasters, Halifaxes and Mosquitoes, including Barton's LK797 'E', were assigned to the task.[3]

The route and return was quite straightforward with no detours; this has since been a point of controversy. Similarly, a late weather forecast gave warning that the outward flight might be made in bright moonlight with no cloud cover, thereby

Barton's new Halifax LK 797 'E'

No. 578 Squadron.   Operational Crew List   30th March 1944.

IMPORTANT. All sections and individuals should check this list as far as possible and any omissions or errors should be brought to the notice of the Squadron Orderly Room immediately.

LW 469	LK "A"	40260	S/L	Harte-Lovelace	A.	Capt.
		1585074	Sgt	Owen	D.	Nav.
		658205	F/S	Collins	J.N.	A/B
		128407	F/L	Gaylor	R.	W/OP.
		1672587	Sgt	Christie	W.	F/E
		1371404	Sgt	McLachlan	A.F.	MU/G
		54179	P/O	Walker	T.B.	R/G
			F/O	Webster		2nd Pilot.
LW 471	LK "D"	1322012	F/S	Malvern	J.A.	Capt.
		R140683	F/S	Morris	G.H.	Nav
		R153903	F/S	Ingleby	W.C.	A/B
		1578731	Sgt	Pountney	W.F.	W/OP
		1581375	Sgt	Dyer	K.	F/E
		970903	Sgt	Murray	R.	MU/G
		1822741	Sgt	Taylor	T.	R/G
LK 797	LK "E"	168669	P/O	Barton	C.J.	Capt.
		1563537	Sgt	Lambert	J.	Nav
		J22053	F/O	Crate	G.	A/B
		169188	P/O	Kay	J.	W/OP
		1676395	Sgt	Trousdale	M.	F/E
		1409549	Sgt	Wood	H.	MU/G
		1850681	Sgt	Brice	F.	R/G
LW 473	LK "F"	1480135	F/S	Henderson	G.M.	Capt.
		573575	F/S	Smith	P.J.	Nav
		1551132	F/S	McDonald	W.W.	A/B
		1218663	Sgt	Whitwell	N.S.	W/OP
		904289	Sgt	Corker	R.C.	F/E
		1658439	Sgt	Wilkenson	W.J.	MU/G
		A488421	F/O	Grey	P.J.	R/G
LV 784	LK "K"	106 2394	F/S	Marsden	G.A.	Capt.
		1320421	F/S	Thomson	R.L.	Nav
		1396837	F/S	Black	R.	A/B
		1458557	Sgt	Rolls	H.	W/OP
		1522197	Sgt	McBrearsy	C.	F/E
		1808453	Sgt	Furner	H.	MU/G
		1815107	Sgt	Farley	N.A.	R/G
LW 675	LK "L"	1339596	Sgt	Edwards	P.	Capt.
		1457472	Sgt	Kendall	H.	Nav
		1353275	Sgt	Flindell	H.T.	A/B
		1249542	Sgt	Young	R.C.	W/OP
		1.	Sgt	Johnson	G.	F/E
		1339700	Sgt	Ferris	L.A.	MU/G
		1468647	Sgt	Harrison	W.	R/G
MZ 513	LK "P"	1433258	Sgt	Clark	M.H.	Capt.
		J21646	F/O	Bower-Binns	J.E.	Nav
		147189	F/L	Hart	F.	A/B
		987547	F/S	Dickson	D.	W/OP
		1400614	Sgt	Richards	W.G.	F/E
		1592964	Sgt	Scorer	J.	MU/G
		952534	Sgt	Roberts	L.	R/G

Operational crew list

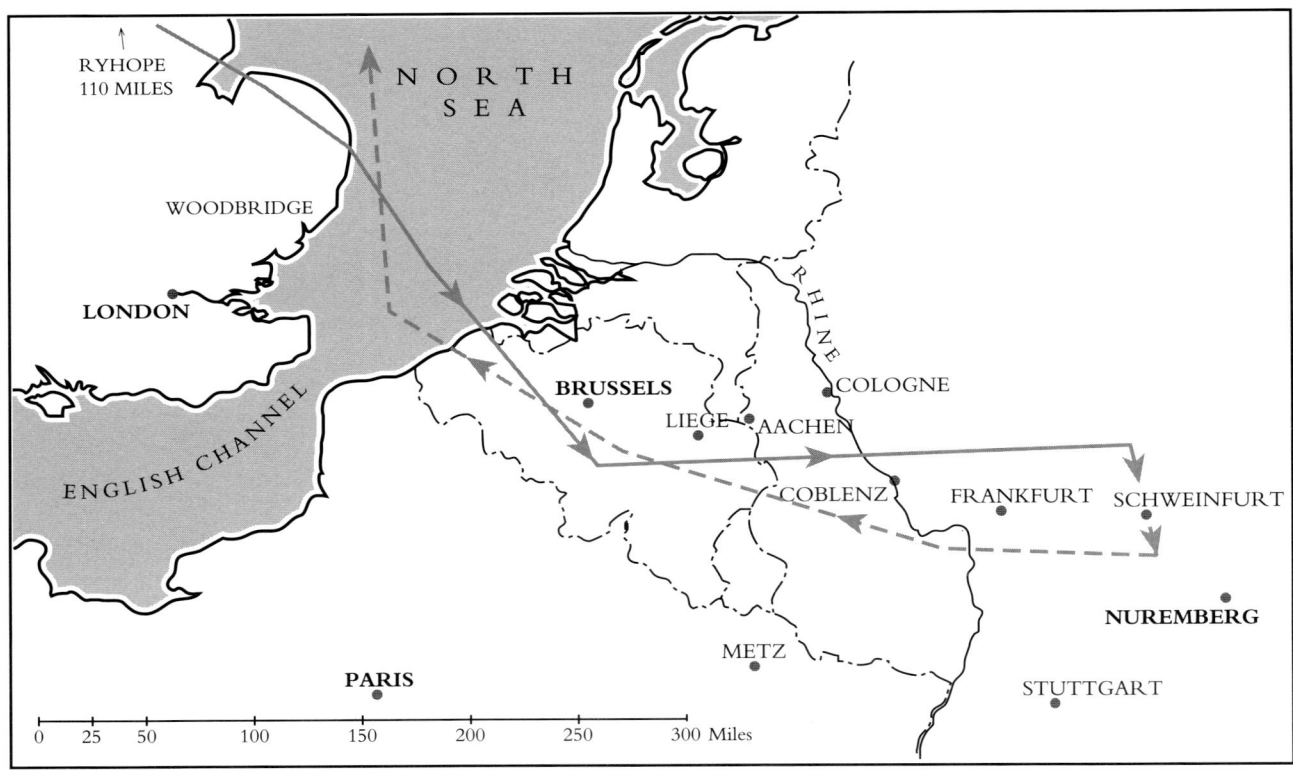

The last flight of Flight path of LK 797 'E'

exposing the bombers to marauding enemy fighters.[4]

Len Lambert, navigator of LK797 'E', recalls:

"I tell you it was a raid which we thought was going to be cancelled. The first thing was that we were forecast to have cloud all the way and in fact it happened the other way about because we had bright moonlight all the way, which is a disaster, and then cloud at the target so that we couldn't see the target properly."[5]

Freddie Brice, rear gunner:

"We took off at 22.12 on the night of 30 March 1944, target: Nuremberg. Once airborne, as usual, we spoke over the intercom only when it was necessary so that all messages got through immediately; Cy did not like idle chatter whilst flying. We had our usual run down through England gaining height all the time. We climbed above what little cloud there was, up into a sky almost as light as day, each with our own thoughts. We crossed the enemy coast . . . We realised it was a night for the night fighter. Several times Cy reminded us to keep our eyes peeled, his voice ever calm over the intercom."[6]

Len Lambert:

"There was a long leg which we had to fly; it really was tremendously long without any deviation until we turned in onto the target. Apart from the lack of cloud cover, the other thing which went wrong was the wind. At the height we were flying, the wind must have reached about 100 mph . . . That meant we were pushed further than originally calculated."[7]

Freddie Brice:
(Halfway along the 'long leg')

"Ahead things began to happen. Two searchlights had snapped on, shining upright in the sky either side of the route we were flying. We passed between them; they did not move. And then ahead again fighter flares began to appear almost like a runway lit up as they were being dropped either side. The bomb aimer reported an

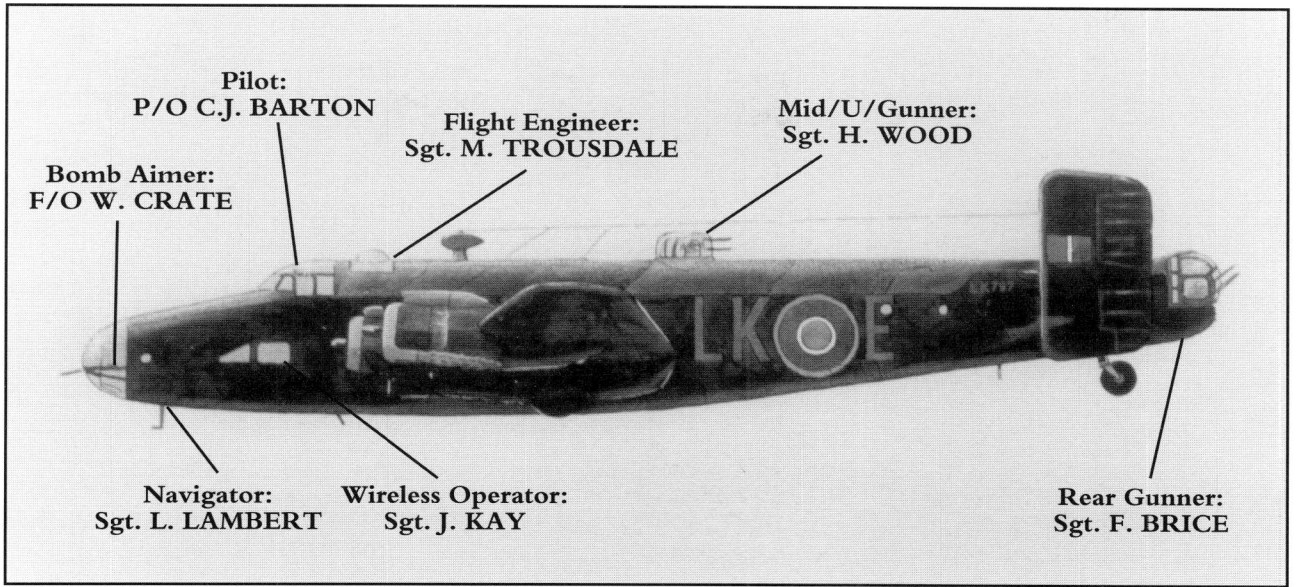

Positions of the crew

aircraft was being attacked ahead, and then yet another. Things were now certainly hotting up. We kept up our search in the sky, wondering as I was, if it would be our turn next; so far we were getting away with it. We came onto our last leg to the target, some 70 miles. The navigator gave his alteration of course, and we began a steep turn to port. We were half-way round when there was a shout from someone. The next thing was a series of bangs up front."[8]

H.D. 'Timber' Wood, mid-upper gunner:

"A voice called out an evasive action command; the Halifax shuddered, dipped into a slight dive and the intercom went dead. Cy took the required corkscrew action, but we had been hit in the starboard inner engine and nose by a Ju88 attacking from the starboard bow. When I heard the evasive action call I rotated my turret, at the same time elevating my four Browning .303 machine guns, and fired blindly to the rear. Only one gun operated: the others were frozen solid. During a turn to port I spotted the Ju88 beneath us and with my one Browning fired a long burst at it, but it flew away out of sight into the darkness. Although we had no way of speaking to each other, we did have an emergency method of communication. By pressing a button it was possible to send messages on an inter-call light. Early in our training days as a crew we had devised our own code, using Morse, to contact each other. The call for Cy to resume course was the letter 'R' or a series of 'dot-dash-dot'; this was transmitted and we resumed course. Moments later the Ju88 reappeared on our port beam, so I punched off a series of dots. This was the signal for Cy to resume his corkscrew action, beginning with a diving turn to port. During this an Me210 joined the fight from up front. I saw its tracer fly harmlessly over our heads to the rear, then caught a brief glimpse of it in silhouette as it sped past on our starboard side and out of sight. We had now lost the Me210 and Ju88, so I sent Cy the 'resume course' signal. He brought the Halifax back to straight and level flight. When first attacked we were at our maximum height; at the end we were down to 9, 000 feet.

Unhappily the bomb aimer, navigator and wireless-operator/air-gunner had misinterpreted one of the inter-call light signals and baled out."[9]

Len Lambert:

"I was in the blacked-out compartment and couldn't see what was going on outside, but,

'For Valour', a painting by K.B. Hancock.

before we were attacked, I could hear reports from members of the crew who were reporting this aircraft on fire, that aircraft on fire and so forth. As soon as the attack began, cannon shells were exploding in my navigator's compartment. It obviously caught a lot of our equipment. I could see some of the electrical equipment was on fire and the great tragedy was that the intercom, the internal telephone, went dead and really that was the greatest problem we had. It has been written that the crew in the forward compartment, the navigator, wireless operator and bomb aimer, misinterpreted the signals and thought it was the order to bale out. That part of the aircraft was on fire at the time and you literally only had seconds to get out if you were really badly hit. Aircraft would be flying along and then you would suddenly see flames licking along the wings where they had been hit and then an almighty bang and that was it, so you really didn't have long. My position as navigator was unfortunate because my seat was over the escape hatch so it was always our drill as we approached the target for me to fold up my seat, clip on my parachute and observe so that if we had to get out quickly I could get the hatch open. What actually happened was that I reached for my parachute and the aircraft was being flung all over the place. Instead of getting it by the handle to lift it out of its rack, I obviously got hold of the rip cord which was a big metal handle and pulled this so that the parachute opened in the aircraft and of course that part of the aircraft was burning at the time so all I could do was to get the part of the parachute which came open and hold it and then try to steady myself on the floor to clear the escape hatch. It was while I was doing this that the escape hatch jammed and I don't know whether someone pushed me or whether it was the aircraft but the next thing I knew I was in mid-air. I didn't jump as such and the other two obviously followed me because they were in the nose of the aircraft. But none of this would have happened if we had had the intercom."[10]

Throughout the fighter attacks, Freddie Brice's gun-firing system had proved to be inoperative. His sense of isolation at the rear of the Halifax became one of fear when "the aircraft began to vibrate badly and sparks began to shoot past my rear turret. Not knowing what was happening up front, I began to wonder if it was time I jumped, but at the same time I thought Cy would do everything possible to let us all know on the call light if he thought there was no hope of coming through, and if he didn't have time then it would be all over quickly".[11]

Barton checked the physical damage to the aircraft with Maurice Trousdale - there was obviously a lot of fuel gone from the two ruptured tanks (some 400 gallons, it was later estimated); one engine was useless; the radio and intercom systems and the rear turret were out of commission; and he was now without navigational or wireless guidance.[12]

'Timber' Wood:

"In spite of this, Cy flew on and bombed the target indicators shining, as we then thought, over Nuremberg; we did not find out until many years later that our bombs were in fact jettisoned on Schweinfurt. The starboard inner engine was by now vibrating furiously; evidently it had been badly damaged. Eventually, its propeller, which was red-hot, tore loose and flew up and away into the night like an enormous Catherine-wheel. The engine did not catch fire, but threw sparks back briefly, then died. After releasing our bomb load, Cy flew well past the blazing target before turning on to a direct heading for home. We had, once before, landed at the emergency aerodrome at Woodbridge and it is likely that Cy had this in mind when setting course. Using his captain's map and steering by the stars and compass he flew the Halifax across enemy territory, avoiding bunches of searchlights en route. During this part of the journey and despite an absence of power from the starboard inner, Cy managed to increase our altitude so that when we crossed the French coast we were at 13,000 feet. We were well into the return journey, when Maurice Trousdale, our flight engineer, came down the fuselage and told me what had been happening. We still had a long way to go and were without three very important members of the crew. My first reaction was to ask about the fuel position and when Maurice told me that we had sufficient to see us back home I opted to press on. Cy and Maurice, too, voted for the return attempt. Shortly after this, I left my turret on instructions from Cy and made my way further down the fuselage to Fred Brice in the rear turret, where I told him of the situation and the decision to carry on."[13]

Freddie Brice:

"It was a great relief to speak to someone . . . I went up front and tapped Cy on the shoulder. He looked round and, with a big grin on his face, gave the thumbs up and said that with a bit of luck we would soon hit the English coast. The mid-upper ('Timber' Wood) was down in the nose looking around so I thought I would join him . . ."[14]

'Timber' Wood:

"The underside of the navigator's desk was badly holed and the maps inside the drawer had been torn to shreds by exploding cannon shells. When I descended the steps into the nose of the aircraft, I was met by a blast of air which came into the Halifax through the square hole in the floor left when the escape hatch was jettisoned during the baling out. It was still dark when we crossed the enemy coast and we then spent a long time over water. Someone suggested that if some searchlights we had avoided earlier on the flight back were surrounding Frankfurt, as we had thought at that time, since we were now heading due west, we could be flying down the English Channel and making for the Atlantic. So in the circumstances Cy decided that we should turn north. Had we but known it, we were at that moment not more than twenty minutes' flying time from the emergency aerodrome at Woodbridge. We maintained the new course until we crossed some lights in the sea, which we took to be convoy marking lights. At this point, Cy returned to a westerly heading. The grey of dawn became brighter and we could make out a Beaufighter flying past. Using the Very pistol, Maurice hurriedly fired off the distress signal, but the Beaufighter pilot, having identified us, flew on into the morning mist and out of sight. Like all Allied aircraft, we carried an IFF set, but this was out of action. We realised later on that the Beaufighter had been sent out to intercept an unidentified aircraft approaching the coast; once he had recognised us, he naturally left us alone. Barrage balloons had also been raised, and although our radio and intercom were not working, we could pick up the distinctive 'squeaker' sound the balloons emitted. The ground defences, however, failed to recognise us and we were fired upon. As a result, Cy turned on to a reciprocal course and flew back out to sea. In the nose, I connected up the Aldis lamp, signalled SOS and a message to say we were friendly. That stopped the firing and I immediately made my way back, carefully avoiding the open escape hatch."[15]

Freddie Brice:

"Cy shouted to me to go back and tell the Engineer to change tanks; he must have noticed a failing in the engines. I dashed back, shouted to Maurice who immediately switched tanks. I then turned to return up front."[16]

'Timber' Wood:

"Just as I reached the cockpit Cy called to me, 'Get aft quickly.' He shouted, 'We're going to crash!' The fuel pipes from one of the petrol tanks had been severed during the attack; when Maurice switched over, the fuel ran out instead of into the engines."[17]

Freddie Brice:

"I met Harry, the 'mid-upper', dashing back. He shouted crash positions, also passing the same message to Maurice on the way. We took up our crash positions, sitting on the floor, with our backs against the rear spar, hands behind our heads. It was not long to wait. There was a bump. The aircraft lurched to starboard and port . . . then a blue flash. The next I remember was a deadly silence. I thought, this is it. It seemed to be daylight but where was I?"[18]

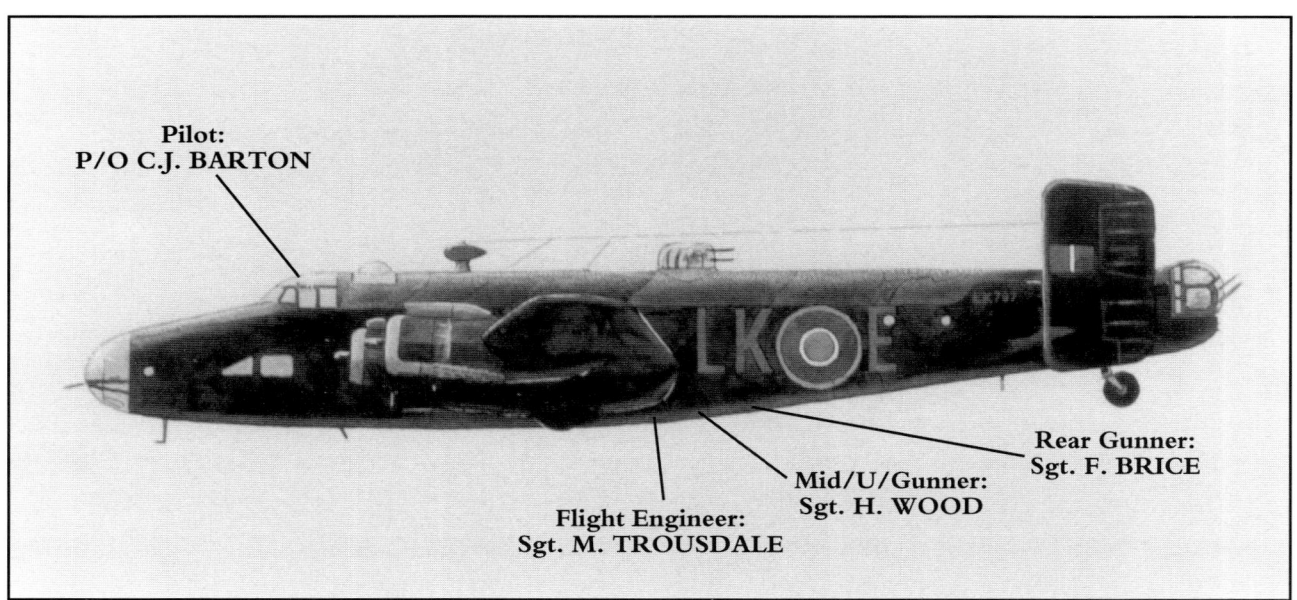

Crash positions on impact at Ryhope

Cherry Knowle Hospital, Ryhope.

'Timber' Wood

"I had just settled in my crash position when the first bump came. I was knocked out. When I came round, it was the sound of Maurice urgently requesting Fred to 'Get off me bloody leg!' I looked over and saw Fred trying to get out of the fuselage through the escape hatch above the crash position."[19]

Freddie Brice:

"I became conscious of faces looking down on me, and I raised myself up and soon willing hands were pulling me out over the wreckage. I was asked how many were in the aircraft, I said four and turned to point to the nose of the aircraft to tell them Cy was there. As I looked, I realised there was no nose left, no wings or engines, just a half of the fuselage in which we had been. We had in fact crashed in the area of a coalmine at Ryhope in Sunderland. The miners were our rescuers. They gave us first aid and we were then admitted to Cherry Knowle Hospital. It was the next day we were to learn that Cy had died on reaching the hospital."[20]

'Timber' Wood:

"From the colliery, we were transferred to Cherry Knowle hospital and placed in the Emergency Ward, where Maurice was given several blood transfusions. Fred and I received treatment for our back injuries. A lasting memory I have is of the kindness of the miners, one of whom was killed and another injured as a result of the crash, and of the nurses under Sister Herbert, who has only just died on 10th April, 1994, aged 79."[21]

PAGE NO: 1

PART I - AIR OPERATIONS

BOMBER COMMAND

1. **30/31 MAR. - NIGHT OPERATIONS**

    934 aircraft, including six U.S. Fortresses, were despatched on the following operations:-

	Pathfinder Force	Main Force
795 on NUREMBERG	110 Lancasters 9 Mosquitos	462 Lancasters 214 Halifaxes
19 on KASSEL ('Spoof')		Mosquitos
9 on COLOGNE ('Spoof')		Mosquitos
55 on Sea-Mining - HELIGOLAND, TEXEL and LE HAVRE		49 Halifaxes 6 Stirlings
6 on AACHEN		Mosquitos
3 on OBERHAUSEN		Mosquitos
2 on JULIANADORP		Mosquitos
1 on DORTMUND		Mosquito
11 on Enemy Airfields		Mosquitos
19 on Intruder Patrols		Mosquitos
14 on Propaganda Leaflets - FRANCE		8 Wellingtons 6 U.S. Fortresses

    655 attacked primary targets and areas
    31 attacked other targets
    8 reports outstanding
    15 carried out Intruder patrols
    54 laid sea-mines
    14 dropped propaganda leaflets
    63 abortive
    94 casualties - no reports

    RESULTS

    NUREMBERG

    608 aircraft, comprising 454 Lancasters, 146 Halifaxes and eight Mosquitos attacked, dropping about 2,148 tons of bombs (967 tons of H.E. and 1,181 tons of incendiaries). Among the H.E. bombs dropped were 6 x 8,000 lb. and 322 x 4,000 lb. Flares were also dropped.
    The Pathfinders were over the target from 0059 hours to 0125 hours, with the Main Force attacking between 0103 and 0135 hours.
    /The

ASO Summary

A.S.O. SUMMARY NO: 1227

TOP SECRET

1 APR. 1944

PAGE NO: 2

B.C. (Contd.)

1. The route to the target was comparatively free from cloud but over the target 6/10ths to 10/10ths cloud in layers up to about 16,000 feet was encountered. Some reports state that the attack opened slightly late and, with marker bombs only occasionally visible through the thinner cloud, most crews bombed on the sky marker flares which are reported as being somewhat scattered with the concentration improving in the later stages of the attack.

The weather conditions made assessment of results difficult but the attack generally appears to have been widely scattered with no extensive area of fire, although a number of fires were seen in the target area and at least three large explosions are reported.

Slight to moderate flak was experienced over the target, with a few ineffective searchlights. Opposition from enemy fighters was strong especially on the route in, and in the target area, and appeared to be particularly severe to the South of the RUHR and in the FRANKFURT area. One Me.110, one Me.109 and one Ju.88 are claimed as destroyed, one Me.110 as probably destroyed and three Ju.88 as damaged.

Of the 795 aircraft despatched on this operation, 64 LANCASTERS (including 11 Pathfinders) and 30 Halifaxes are missing. One Halifax crashed at WATLINGTON (all crew killed) one at SILVERSTONE (four killed) and one at RYHOPE near SUNDERLAND (three of crew baled out over target and one was killed in the crash). A Lancaster crashed at WELFORD (all crew killed) and another at LANDBEACH (two killed). In addition one Halifax crashed in the sea about 60 miles South of SELSEY BILL, six of the crew being rescued but the pilot is missing.

Other Targets

29 aircraft, comprising 24 Lancasters, four Halifaxes and one Mosquito attacked a variety of targets in the LOW COUNTRIES and Western GERMANY.

KASSEL ('Spoof').

19 Mosquitos attacked between 0024 and 0030 hours from 21,000 to 25,000 feet dropping about 20 tons of H.E. (including 8 x 4,000 lb.) and 7 x 250 lb. marker bombs in conditions of 3/10ths to 10/10ths cloud with tops at 6,000 to 9,000 feet and good visibility. Markers were well concentrated, bursts were seen through cloud and a large explosion is reported in the target area.

Very slight spasmodic and inaccurate heavy flak was encountered.

COLOGNE ('Spoof').

Nine Mosquitos attacked from 24,000 to 32,000 feet dropping about 12 tons of H.E. (including 5 x 4,000 lb.) and 1 x 250 lb. marker bomb in conditions of nil to 2/10ths cloud and considerable ground haze. Slight to moderate heavy flak was experienced with about 60 searchlights coning.

References

[1] *Cyril Barton's flight log book*
[2] *Interview with Alan Mitcheson, 8th October, 1993*
[3] *Air Staff Operational Summary, 1st April, 1944 (NB There is some debate as to the number of aircraft involved. For example, Geoffrey Jones' 'Raider' gives a figure of 779 bombers)*
[4] *Geoffrey Jones: 'Raider', p. 121*
[5] *Interview with Len Lambert, 7th November, 1993*
[6] *Letter from F. Brice to Sgt. Bowyer, 1st December, 1968*
[7] *Interview with Len Lambert, 7th November, 1993*
[8] *Letter from F. Brice, 1st December, 1968*
[9] *Geoffrey Jones: 'Raider', pp. 123-4*
[10] *Interview with Len Lambert, 7th November, 1993*
[11] *Letter from F. Brice, 1st December, 1968*
[12] *Chaz Bowyer: 'For Valour: The Air VCs', p. 356*
[13] *Geoffrey Jones: 'Raider', pp. 124-5*
[14] *Letter from F. Brice, 1st December, 1968*
[15] *Geoffrey Jones: 'Raider' p.126*
[16] *Letter from F. Brice, 1st December, 1968*
[17] *Geoffrey Jones: 'Raider,' p. 126*
[18] *Letter from F. Brice, 1st December, 1968*
[19] *Geoffrey Jones: 'Raider', p. 126*
[20] *Letter from F. Brice, 1st December, 1968*
[21] *Geoffrey Jones: 'Raider,' p. 126*

Chapter 4

The View from Ryhope

5 Ludlow Road,

Sunderland.

Co. Durham.

28th June, 1944.

Mrs. Barton,
New Malden,
Surrey.

Dear Madam,

      I trust you will not think it intrusion on my part in my writing you in this your hour of trial and trouble. When reading this morning's Press I observe that it was your son who crashed within a mile of my home on the morning of March 31st, and I thought you might like to have some first-hand information from one who watched his 'plane cross our coast till the unfortunate moment when he was taken to the Great Beyond.

      The sirens had been sounded at 5.25 a.m. and being a member of the A.R.P. Services I dressed immediately and reported to my Assembly Point. We had only been on duty a few minutes when we observed a heavy bomber cross our coast about a mile away. Immediately on reaching land coloured flares were dropped from the 'plane - apparently to convey that it was one of our own 'planes. We soon realised that the 'plane was in difficulties by the sound of its engines, and flying rather low, the 'plane came inland about a mile and a half, and twice circled two hills immediately in front of my home about half a mile away. On circling to the right he came over towards the centre of our town and we had the impression that he had sighted the balloon barrage and turned again inland.

      The All Clear had now been sounded at 5.40 a.m., and we were making for our respective homes; I myself had just gone indoors when we heard the terrific roar of the bomber making towards my home. My wife and I rushed to the door and we were actually within hailing distance of the 'plane as he passed overhead. My neighbour next door who is a Warden and I ran over the fields feeling certain that the plane would crash in our immediate vicinity. It went on, however, a mile and a half away and came down quite close to Ryhope Colliery, which is outside the boundary of Sunderland. So I was not present at the actual scene of the crash.

      We can only mourn the passing of such brave boys, and my wife joins with me in sending you our very deepest sympathy.

Yours sincerely,

Wm Asquith

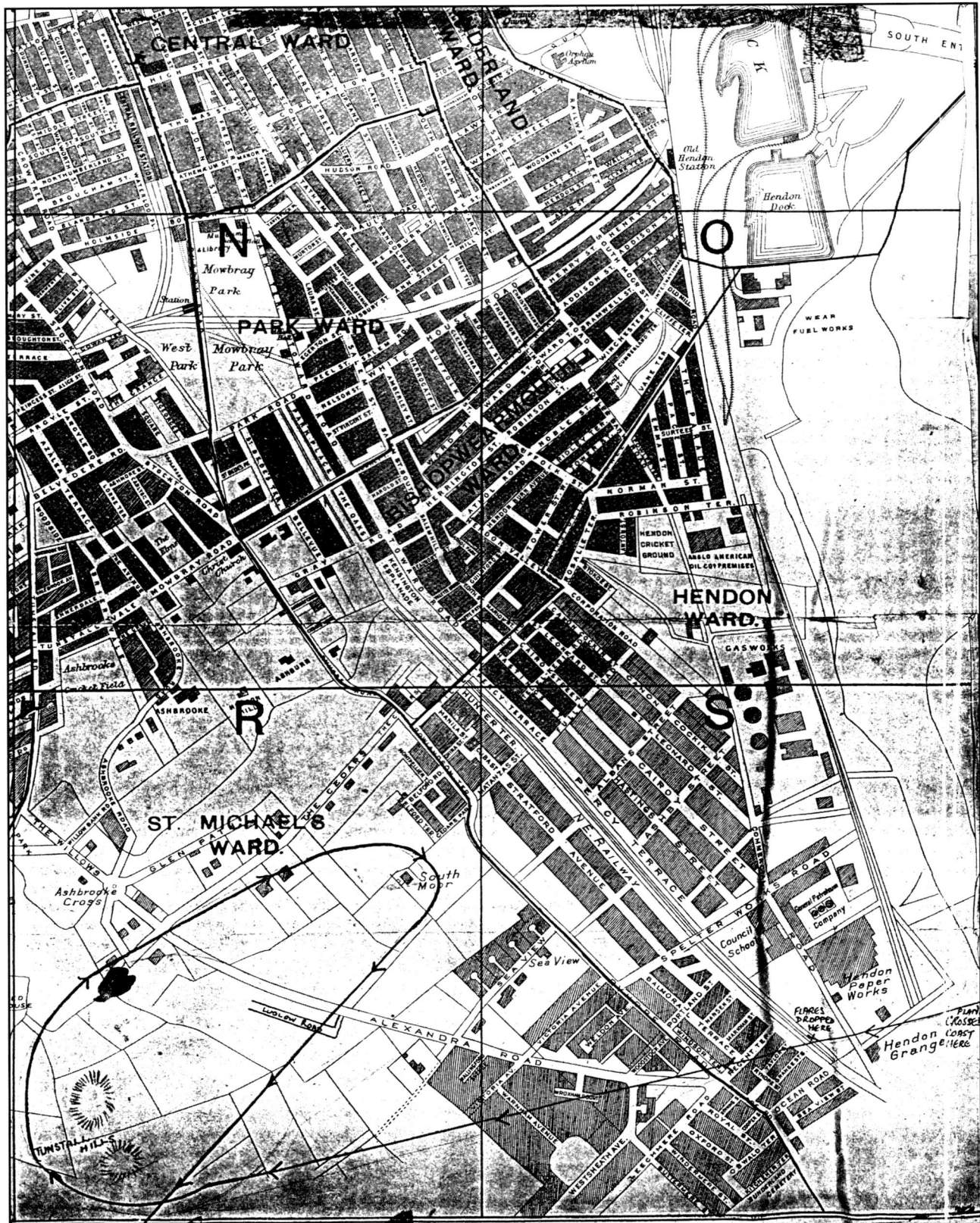

This map accompanied Mr. Asquith's letter

Les Lawther:
(A miner at Ryhope Colliery):

"I was working permanent night shift and I used to finish at five o'clock in the morning. That morning, it was my turn to examine the water stapple (pump) in the yard . . . I had to wait for the engine man to lower me down to do the examination then come up to sign the book. He didn't come on until seven o'clock. I was waiting in the shaft cabin and the sirens went . . . well really it was a buzzer. I went to the reservoir. Just below this was the spotter shed built into the side of the hill . . . The cabin was a special place, built for spotting 'planes during the war. There were telephones there . . . Jack Coxon was the ['plane] spotter . . . There was a spotter there twenty-four hours a day.

I was standing at the door and the 'All Clear' sirens had gone. There was this 'plane coming in . . . When I was standing in the doorway, on my right was the colliery, my left was Silksworth. Jack Coxon said, 'It's one of ours'. Mind, he was very low and only had two propellers running, all on one side . . . Now when that 'plane came in, there was somebody on that 'plane flashed a light, and he went up over the main road (Ryhope to Silksworth) and he came back the way he came in . . . He went a bit far towards Silksworth, round the back of the big stone heap and away out to sea again."[1]

Tom Richardson:
(He lived at number one, West Terrace, Ryhope; he was 16 years old at the time).

"On the morning of the crash, we were in bed and we were woken by the sirens. It must have been between five and six. My mother, younger brother and myself went out to the Anderson Shelter. We were in the air-raid shelter for about half an hour; the All Clear went at six - it was just breaking daylight. My mother and brother went inside the house next to the fireplace; I was stood on the front doorstep on the corner of the house and was talking to the man next door but one. I saw the 'plane go behind the pit and it went out to sea and we lost sight of him. I could not tell whether he was in trouble or even if it was a British 'plane."[2]

Alan Mitcheson:
(He lived in Hewitt Avenue and was almost 12 years old at the time.)

"I hadn't been in bed long, and in fact was almost asleep, when I heard the sound of an aircraft. By the sound of its engines, I guessed it was one of ours. In wartime, one got used to distinguishing the difference in the drone between RAF and German aircraft. However, the artillery at the top of our street at Leechmere, behind Tom Hall's hostel, began to fire their anti-aircraft guns. I looked out of my bedroom window, which faced the coast, and could see a large aircraft travelling north towards the gasometers at Hendon. It turned inland and seemed to be heading toward Tunstall Hills. At the time I was somewhat confused as to why the guns were firing *after* the All-Clear sirens had sounded. A few minutes later I heard it coming back and fading into the distance."[3]

Les Lawther cannot remember hearing the guns firing at the 'plane. It was pointed out to him that

Les Lawther

some accounts record that the Leechmere Battery fired on the 'plane.

Les Lawther:

"They were big guns and when they went off they shook the house."

Les's wife, Florence, was present at the interview. During the war, she was in the army and at one time was based at the Leechmere Battery.

Florence Lawther:

"There was a tracer gun in that command post as well as the big guns. There was always somebody on the tracer gun. I was not there that night, but somebody could have fired the tracer gun, thinking it was the enemy, it was that low."

Les Lawther:

"The tracer gun didn't make as much noise as the big guns."[4]

Alan Mitcheson:

"Some ten minutes or so later, I was awakened yet again by the sound of the aircraft, only this time it sounded different. I got up to look out of the window and couldn't believe my eyes. It was much lower and port and starboard navigation lights were on. It was approaching from a southerly direction and the engines were making a spluttering sound, like when a car misfires. It was obviously in trouble as it got nearer, so I jumped out of bed and ran across to my parents' room. It passed over our rooftops and started to fall over the houses in front of me, as it did so, it banked slightly to the left before hitting the end house of West Terrace, on what was then known as Vinegar Hill. This was accompanied by a noise like thunder."[5]

Les Lawther:

"Now when he came in the next time . . . From where I was standing, there was the spotter's

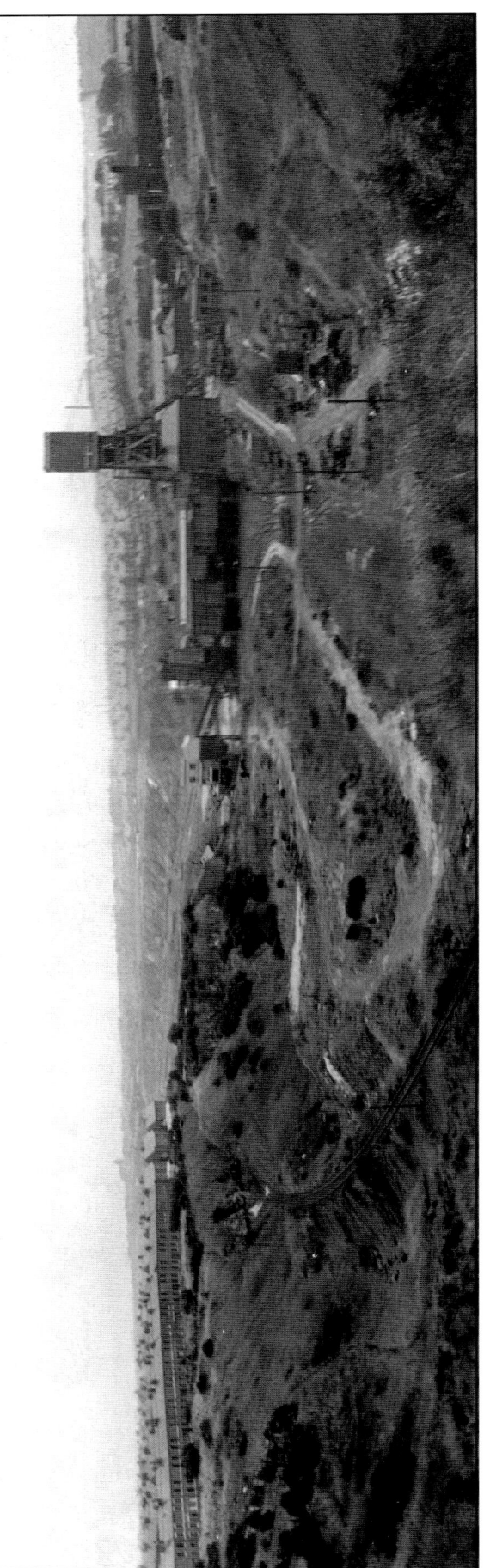

Ryhope Colliery and the crash site

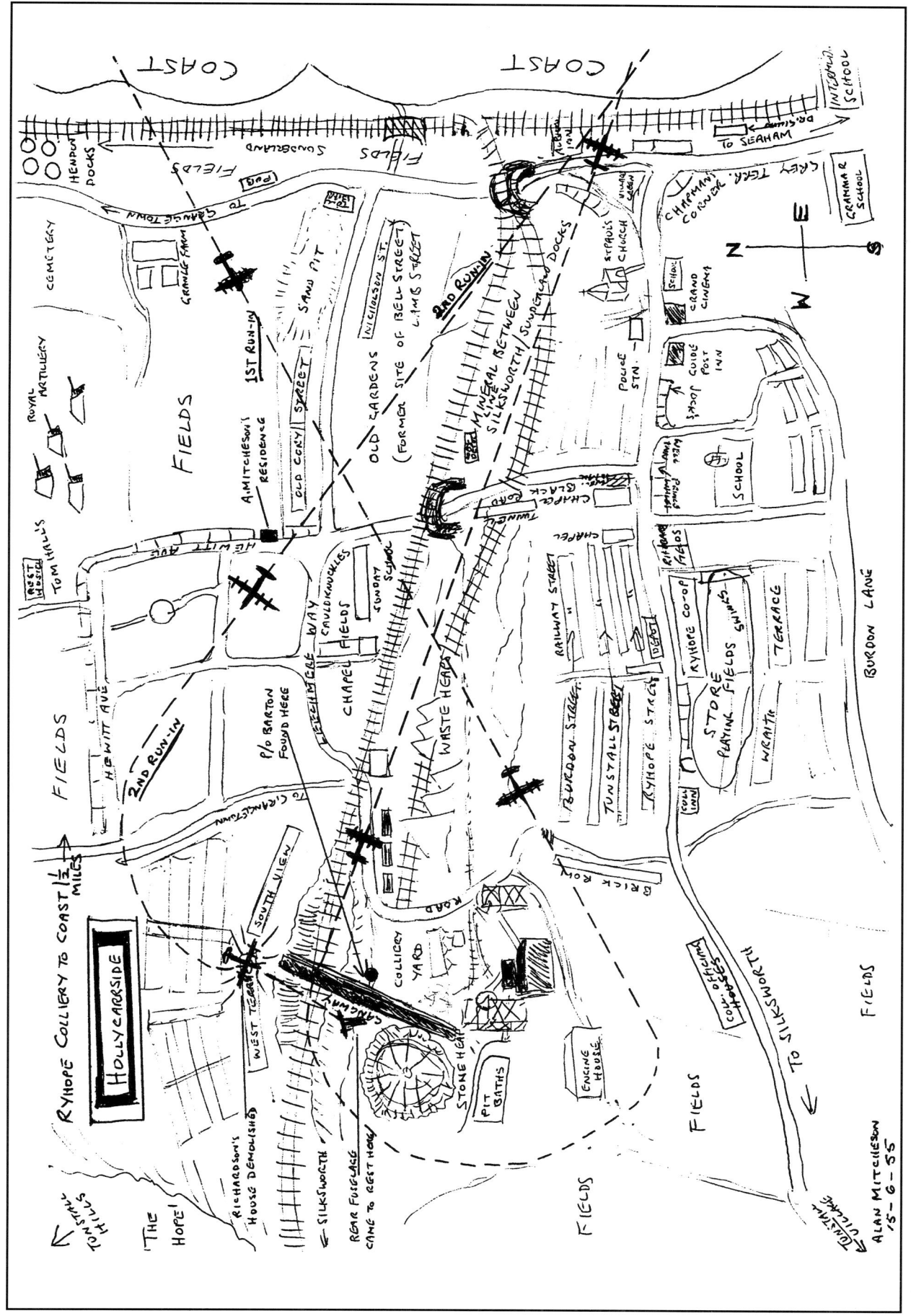

Alan Mitcheson's map of the crash site

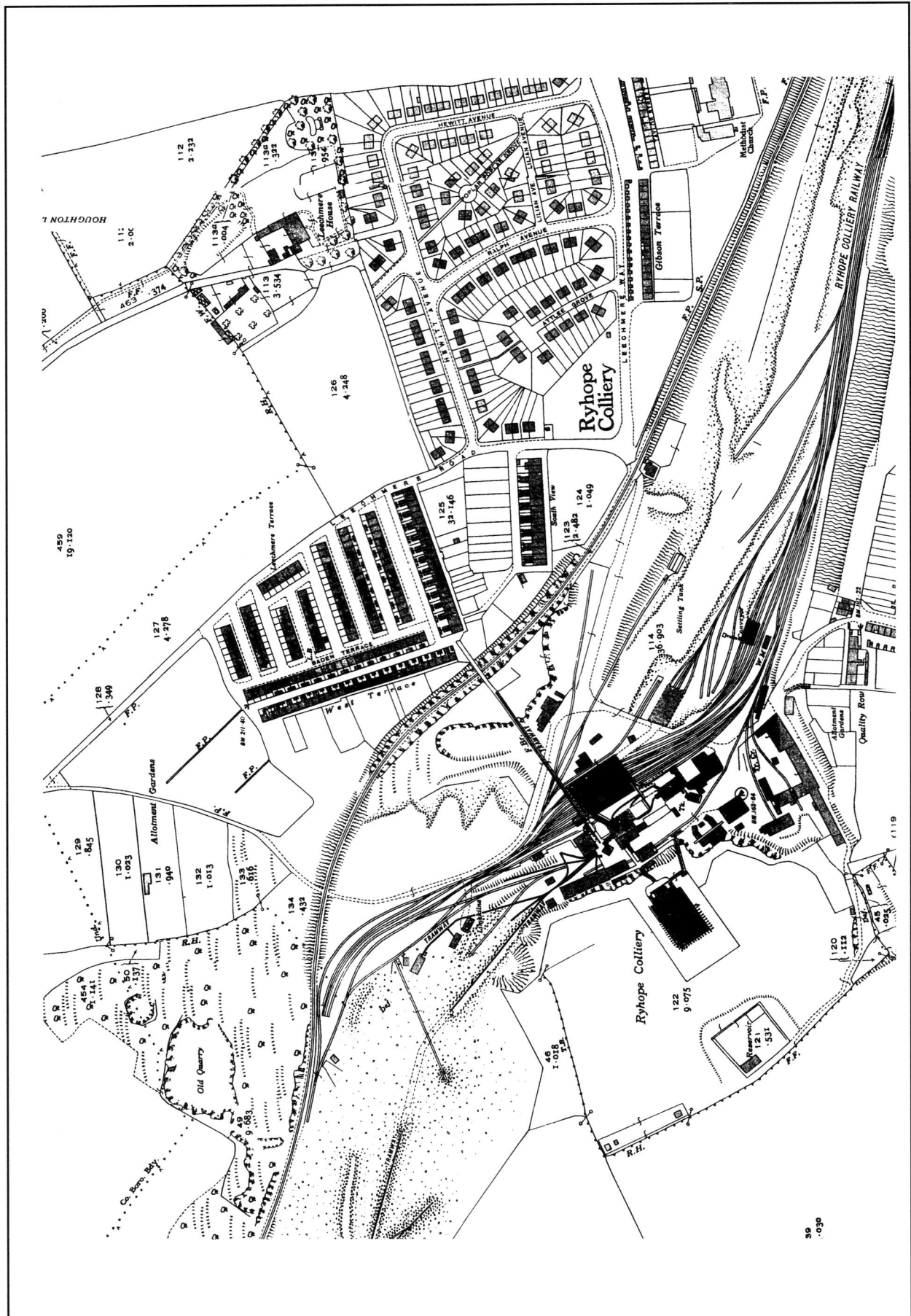

1939 OS map of Ryhope and the colliery (Crown copyright)

shed, the reservoir, and the head gear (in line). It was a morning where it wasn't really misty, but it had a bit of haze . . . I contend he saw the headgear, because he was very low, and naturally he tried to avoid it. But he was too near to get round and his wing just caught the end house on West Terrace and the plane just tumbled . . . If he went the other way, he would have hit the house on Hollycarr Terrace."[6]

Arthur Milburn:

"I was seventeen years old at the time of the 'plane crash. I lived in Ryhope at 4, Leechmere Road. I heard the 'plane at about six o'clock in the morning. I came out of the house and went down the path and saw the aircraft approaching. A bit frightened that it was enemy aircraft, I dashed back towards the door, turned round, and saw it going down between the houses of Hollycarr Terrace and Powell Terrace, catching the houses on each side with its wings then eventually hitting the end house of West Terrace, which was the house of the Richardson family. It came to rest on the gardens just adjacent to the colliery. I heard an almighty crash; there was no fire or explosions, just the crash and rumble of buildings being demolished."[7]

Tom Richardson:

"I just stepped one step off the step and heard what sounded like a rushing wind, getting louder. The first thing we had been told to do was dive at the side of a wall which is the safest place. There was one hell of a bang and the dust cleared, most of the house was gone, including the front door and the step that I had been standing on. The front wall was swaying and bricks flew overhead. My mother and brother inside were buried, the ceiling came down on top of them, but luckily all the brickwork seemed to be carried away from the house with the debris. The wardens wouldn't let me go in and dragged me out.

Beds were hanging out of the bedrooms, out of the side of the house next to number two. The stairs were at the side of the house on the gable end. My grandfather died 6-9 months before this happened. As he used to sleep under the stairs he would have been killed. The table cloth was found under the 'plane wings. Also, there was a wireless set found with a half brick in the back of the set, but the back was still on. Nobody could ever find out how the brick got in; the back was still screwed on. My father had taken the back off the radio to see why it wasn't working and found the half brick. The warden might have pushed the back on when carrying stuff out. The furniture and everything went as you can imagine.

The 'plane came from the sea and hit the chimney pot in Powell Terrace on the corner. The nose piece of the 'plane was left in the garden and the rest of the 'plane landed in horse manure – this cushioned the fall for the rest of the crew. We were told by RAF personnel that when the 'plane hit the house, the wing must have dipped and the 'plane carried on through a small gap. The engine and the tail flew through the air and came off; the two wings were lying in the garden."[8]

Ken Richardson:

(*He lived at 1, West Terrace and was nine years old at the time.*)

"When the All-Clear went we went back into the house. Me and my mother came in and my brother stayed outside, talking to neighbours. My mother went to put the kettle on, and that was it. Everything came down. After that, every time my mother heard a plane she grabbed anybody. I cannot remember much of it, but what I can remember was a lot of hissing, probably electric and gas. My brother thought it was another bomb going off. As we were standing next to the fireplace, that was the only wall left, we were thrown in the corner next to the window. When we got up, the window was directly in front of us and my mother pushed me through the window to the men outside. Then two of them walked round and had to take her fingers off the window sill, she wouldn't leave go. After that, it was all cleaned up. There was plaster and bricks and lots of dust. We had a built-in cupboard which went from the fireplace to the window wall and we had the wireless on top of there. There was a half-brick went into the back of the wireless. We didn't know until we took the back off. It wouldn't go through the hole; it must have blasted it and expanded, gone in and closed up again. The window was 5–6 feet high and three feet wide. Glass was out and just the frame standing. From the chimney breast wall, there was only about four feet of the house left; all the rest had gone. There were two bedrooms above; they were completely off altogether. My Grandfather had a bed under the stairs in the sitting-room. He had died shortly before, which was just as well; he would have died then in any case. We were on a gable end."[9]

Les Lawther:

"As soon as I saw it hit the house, I ran from the spotter's shed and went to the tail end of the plane. I could hear somebody moaning. The back end of the plane was all broken off and was all open . . . It was lying partly on the gangway and partly on the pit ponies' muck heap . . . There was no trouble getting them out. I got in the plane and helped one out; he walked out like . . . I said, 'Sit there and keep quiet' . . . and went back and got the other one out . . . Now I can't remember a third; I can't remember if there was two or three. Anyway, I got them out and by then Harry Hicks, the ambulance driver, came out to have a look. I told him to get the ambulance and he came round with the colliery ambulance. It was there in a couple of minutes; the ambulance depot was only about 20 steps away; he only had to get it out and back it up . . . The men walked into the ambulance and he took them up to Ryhope Hospital.

"The crew were in shock. All they said to me was, 'Get the pilot' . . . I got back in again. I knew

One of the engines fell onto the railway tracks.

where the pilot would sit, but the front end was missing. There were some men on the gangway then and I said, 'Will you have a look in the gardens to see if you can see the pilot?' They were away a minute or two and they came back and said, 'He's over the bankside on the cliffside, but we can't get him.' So I said, 'Go down to the shaft cabin. The door's still open and there's any amount of ropes. Fetch the lot up'.

Anyway, they ran down and got the ropes and came up. I don't know who the men were, but they lowered down and fetched his body up. Now I don't know how he got to hospital, whether the ambulance went up for him or not, I don't know."[10]

Alan Mitcheson:

"Cyril Barton was carried from the wreckage by marine John Douglas, who was on leave at the time."[11]

13 May 1944	From:
	Dr. J. Bain Alderson
	Ashburne Villa
	Colliery Road
Tel: Ryhope 220	Ryhope Co. Durham

"Dear Mrs. Barton,

Your letter has been forwarded to me by Dr. Gillan, the Ryhope Colliery Surgeon. It was I who attended at the scene of the crash. Your son had sustained injuries to the head and had lost a good deal of blood so I did not attempt to give any treatment but sent him off to hospital at once as I thought a blood transfusion was needed. I understand that he did not regain consciousness after the crash. He was insensible when I saw him; he was not burnt in any way as the plane only burnt a little and the crew were pulled out without any burns.

I very much regret that the hospital authorities and myself were unable to do any more for him.

I shall pass on your thanks to the Civil Defence for the wreath. Please accept also my personal sympathies in your great loss.

Yours faithfully
J. BAIN ALDERSON

"P.S. Name of colliery worker killed was Geo. Heads, South View, Ryhope."

George Heads, a surface engineman of Ryhope Colliery, had, in fact, been on his way to work when he decided to return home.

Les Lawther:

"George Heads lived in the first street facing the colliery, South View . . . The sirens went so he went back 'cause his wife was a bit hard of hearing and I think a bit unsteady. He took his wife to the air-raid shelter, somewhere along their street. He then went down over the gangway. George Heads must have been on the gangway when the plane hit the house and turned over, or whatever it did . . . and the wing fell on him. They didn't know if there was anyone under it and it was obstructing where the men walked. They lifted it up towards the railings, and when they lifted it up he was underneath it."[12]

Tom Richardson:

"George Heads was very unlucky – he was halfway to work when the All-Clear went, about 6 o'clock; he returned to his house, as he was only a few minutes away, to tell his wife that the All-Clear had gone as she was hard of hearing. When he went to go to work the second time was when the plane hit, and they found him under the tail plane dead – he was killed outright."[13]

Arthur Milburn:

"I left the house and ran along South View towards where the plane was. When I got there, there was quite a number of people beyond the

X marks the area where LK 797 'E' came to rest. Richardson's house (off left) was demolished at the end of West Terrace by the falling aircraft. The railway track through the ravine on the left is now filled in.

Richardson house on the side of the colliery. They were trying to lift up a wing. The fuselage itself had broken off and gone into the manure heap, the tail-fin had crashed just on the edge of the gangway and later we found Mr. Heads underneath, who had died . . . It was on the section of the gangway beyond West Terrace, over the cutting and just before the drop to the colliery.

I didn't get near the cockpit; there were quite a few people assisting . . . The authorities came on the scene and we had a wander round and had a look at the fuselage which was in the manure heap. I saw the tail-plane but I don't think anyone noticed Mr. Heads until quite some considerable time after, when he was missing from work. It was the tail-plane which killed him, the two pieces with the piece going across and two supports on the side. They were just on the side of the gangway. . . . I was quite surprised when I just came round the corner of Hollycarr Terrace and was confronted by the heap of rubble which was

Severed main plane section next to the gangway leading to Ryhope Colliery

Alan Mitcheson and George Goldsbrough c.1945

the Richardson house . . . There was just the window-frame. I was surprised that anyone could get out alive. It was just one heap of rubble. I did see Tom later on and he told me that the family were Okay, which surprised me."[14]

Alan Mitcheson:

"Before going to school, me and George Goldsborough went up to the colliery yard. The area below the gangway, next to the ambulance station, was cordoned off by a rope and patrolled by an RAF crash guard from Usworth RAF Station. We then made our way around by the prop yard and up the bank towards South View. When we reached the end of the street near to where the demolished house was, we were told by another crash-guard to keep back behind the rope. He was guarding one of the bomber engines, which was completely blackened as if it had been burning. The propeller blades were twisted and bent.

Almost all of the house was down, certainly

Port wing and engine.

Rear fuselage shortly before salvage operations, end of April, 1944. The schoolboy, bottom right, is Alan Mitcheson.

the gable-end was just a pile of bricks. The severed nose section, what was left of it, was at the bottom of Richardson's garden, another engine in Paxton's garden, and the rear fuselage across the ravine on the hillside facing the colliery yard and next to the gangway."[15]

Tom Richardson:

"My father was at work on a job which he couldn't leave. When the crash happened, he was on his own manning the telephones. 'Phones were vital at the colliery because men's lives were at risk. He couldn't leave the' phones, they were so important. He knew the crash had happened but could not get out of the cabin. His job during the war was patrolling stone heaps and keeping fires down. He had been asked to stand by in the cabin for a while by the telephones.

The man who relieved my father didn't see him leave, he was that quick; he left as soon as he got sight of him. My father came back to what was left of the house and by that time we were wandering about in a daze. He couldn't get back as the engine and tail-plane were blocking the way. The RAF were on the scene and had it partitioned and railed off. We lost furniture and everything – nothing was salvaged. The pantry was next door to No. 2. There must have been such a sharp impact and yet the inside of the pantry was hardly touched. The warden found 12–15 eggs in a dish not even cracked and when he got outside, he fell

'Bella'

and dropped them! This helped to snap us all out of it."

Ken recalls how the fireplace had survived and that the kettle boiled furiously amidst the debris.

"We had a spaniel dog at the time, a bitch called Bella; she was buried under all the debris. In the excitement and shock, we had forgotten about her. Hours later, the warden found her buried under bricks, still alive, but after that the dog was never the same and we lost her within six months.

People were very good and helped one another – within an hour, we got a key for another identical house in Nicholson Street which was meant for another colliery worker. He gave the key up to house us as he already had a house. The family was rehoused in 44, Nicholson Street.

Mr. & Mrs. Barton came to the scene of the crash. My mother and Mrs. Barton corresponded after that for some time. We have a framed

Ken, Rose and Tom Richardson outside their new home in Nicholson Street

photograph of Cyril Barton – 22 years old."[16]

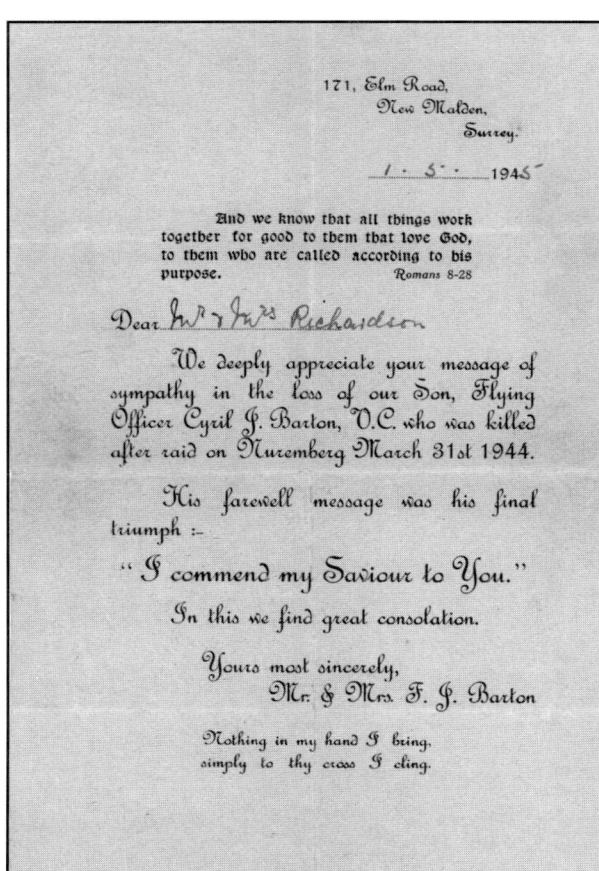

References

[1] Interview with Les Lawther, 19th January, 1994
[2] Interview with Tom Richardson, 12th November, 1993
[3] Alan Mitcheson's letter, dated 26th January, 1994 (in possession of W.W. Lowther)
[4] Interview with Les Lawther, 19th January, 1994
[5] Alan Mitcheson's letter, 26th January, 1994
[6] Interview with Les Lawther, 19th January, 1994
[7] Interview with Arthur Milburn, 28th January, 1994
[8] Interview with Tom Richardson, 12th November, 1993
[9] Interview with Ken Richardson, 8th October, 1993
[10] Interview with Les Lawther, 19th January, 1994
[11] Alan Mitcheson's letter, 26th January, 1994
[12] Interview with Les Lawther, 19th January, 1994
[13] Interview with Tom Richardson, 12th November, 1993
[14] Interview with Arthur Milburn, 28th January, 1994
[15] Alan Mitcheson's letter, 26th January, 1994
[16] Interview with Tom Richardson, 12th November, 1993

Chapter 5

Aftermath – New Malden

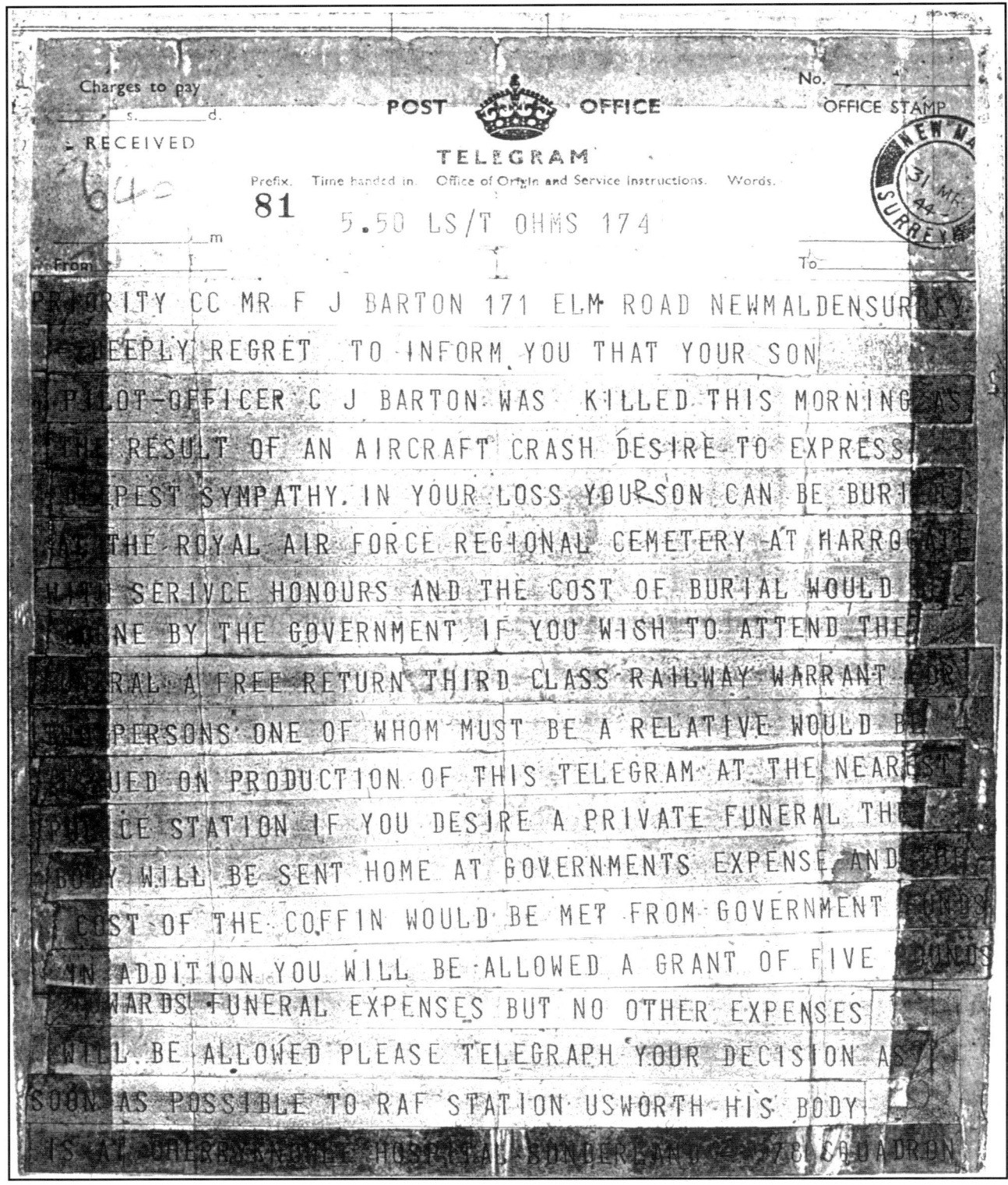

Joyce:

"I was there when the telegram came. It must have been seven o'clock in the evening, a Friday night . . . Mum knew something was wrong . . . She opened the telegram and there were three pages in it . . . and the last one had FUNERAL written . . . and she knew this was it."

Cynthia :

"As we stood there, stunned, Joyce said, 'Don't worry, Mum, he's only gone to live with Jesus'.

The telegram not only informed Mum of Cyril's death, but went on to suggest where he could be buried and what kind of railway ticket she could use if the funeral should be held in the North . . . all in one telegram. Mum was devastated."

Joyce:

"My brother, Roy, came in. He would be about sixteen and Mum said to him to go and fetch Dad and Uncle Reg. Next morning, I remember having to go up to the post office with telegrams made out to let other relatives know . . . we didn't have telephones in those days . . .

His funeral was on Maundy Thursday which was the day after my birthday, April 6th. The coffin was late coming . . . A friend of Cyril's, Frank Colquhoun, was at the service. He was the curate in charge of the church. Cynthia went to the service but Mum wouldn't let Pam and me go. I went next door and peeped through the curtains to see the coffin . . . draped in a Union Jack."[1]

Frank Colquhoun:

"The funeral service was held at his old church, St. John's, New Malden, on the Thursday before Easter, April 6th, 1944. In a brief address at the service I spoke simply of Cyril's radiant Christian character and his shining faith in our Lord; and I reminded those present that Cyril's last flight was not downward but upward. While his plane crashed to earth, his spirit flew straight into the arms of God . . .

We sang the hymns 'When I survey the wondrous cross' and 'Abide with me'. Afterwards, amid the loveliness of the budding spring, we laid the dear remains to rest in a quiet corner of Kingston cemetery."[2]

Cynthia:

"The service was an awful experience for Mum. She had to support Dad through it. He really didn't cope that day at all. He didn't know what he was doing. It was awful."

Joyce:

"It's a good job Mum was the strong character she was, because not only did she have to look after us but she had to hold Dad up as well . . . she had a lot to contend with. My Aunt said that the only dry eye in the church was my mother's."

Cynthia:

"Dad had a great personality . . . but he wasn't strong-willed . . . perhaps this explains why Cyril was such a father figure to us girls.

After Cyril's death . . . Mum's health deteriorated but she was incredible the way she kept going . . . Dad just couldn't pull himself together . . . he just fell apart. He almost became an old man overnight.

We didn't talk about Cyril's death afterwards because we thought it would upset Mum. It must have been about eighteen months later: I came into the house and Mum called out, 'Is that you Cyril?' . . . she was washing in the kitchen. I didn't understand what was going on and when I asked her why she had said that she just broke down and said 'You know, you don't talk about him . . . and I want you to talk about him' . . . So we did after that. We hadn't previously, not because we had forgotten him, rather we didn't want anyone to break down."[3]

No. 578 Squadron,
R.A.F. Station, BURN, Nr. Selby,
Yorks.

578S/C.202/21/P1.   1st April 1944.

Dear Mr. Barton

It is with very deep regret that I have to write and confirm the news already conveyed to you by telegram that your son, Pilot Officer C.J. Barton, has been killed in an aircraft crash. He was one of my most experienced Captains, and led one of my finest crews. His loss leaves a gap in our ranks which it will be impossible to fill.

He and his crew left this Station on the night of the 30th/31st March to attack an important target in Germany. All we know at the moment is that his aircraft sustained serious damage, but despite this, he flew it back to this country then, unfortunately, he crashed soon after crossing our coast.

He always showed a devotion to duty and a keeness which was an example to us all, and you may be proud of the fact that he died doing a magnificent job of work.

His belongings have been collected by one of my Officers and sent to the R.A.F. Central Depository, who will communicate with you in due course.

Please accept the sincere sympathy of myself and all my Squadron in your sad loss, and I would like to tell you that Cyril will never be forgotten by any of his comrades here.

Yours very sincerely,

Wing Commander, Commanding,
No. 578 Squadron,   R.A.F.

Mr. F.J. BARTON,
171, Elm Road,
NEW MALDEN, Surrey.

Extract from "The London Gazette" of 27th June, 1944

"Pilot Officer Cyril Joe Barton (168669) R.A.F.V.R., No. 578 Squadron (Deceased).

ON the night of 30th March, 1944, Pilot Officer Barton was captain and pilot of a Halifax aircraft detailed to attack Nuremberg. When some 70 miles short of the target, the aircraft was attacked by a Junkers 88. The first burst of fire from the enemy made the intercommunication system useless. One engine was damaged when a Messerschmitt 210 joined in the fight. The bomber's machine guns were out of action and the gunners were unable to return the fire.

Fighters continued to attack the aircraft as it approached the target area and, in the confusion caused by the failure of the communications system at the height of the battle, a signal was misinterpreted and the navigator, air bomber and wireless operator left the aircraft by parachute.

Pilot Officer Barton faced a situation of dire peril. His aircraft was damaged, his navigational team had gone and he could not communicate with the remainder of the crew. If he continued his mission, he would be at the mercy of hostile fighters when silhouetted against the fires in the target area, and if he survived he would have to make a $4\frac{1}{2}$ hours journey home on three engines across heavily-defended territory. Determined to press home his attack at all costs, he flew on and, reaching the target, released the bombs himself.

As Pilot Officer Barton turned for home the propeller of the damaged engine, which was vibrating badly, flew off. It was also discovered that two of the petrol tanks had suffered damage and were leaking. Pilot Officer Barton held to his course and, without navigational aids and in spite of strong head winds, successfully avoided the most dangerous defence areas on his route. Eventually he crossed the English coast only 90 miles north of his base.

By this time the petrol supply was nearly exhausted. Before a suitable landing place could be found, the port engine stopped. The aircraft was now too low to be abandoned successfully. Pilot Officer Barton therefore ordered the three remaining members of his crew to take up their crash stations. Then, with only one engine working, he made a gallant attempt to land clear of the houses over which he was flying. The aircraft finally crashed and Pilot Officer Barton lost his life, but his three comrades survived.

Pilot Officer Barton had previously taken part in four attacks on Berlin and 14 other operational missions. On one of these two members of his crew were wounded during a determined effort to locate the target despite the appalling weather conditions. In gallantly completing his last mission in the face of almost impossible odds, this officer displayed unsurpassed courage and devotion to duty.

Tel.: Holborn 3434. Extn. 242.
Communications relating to this letter should be addressed to:—
The Under Secretary of State
quoting:— S.95403/S.10 A
Your Ref. ....

AIR MINISTRY,
LONDON, W.C.2.

26th June, 1944.

Sir,

I am commanded by the Air Council to inform you that the King has been graciously pleased to confer the Victoria Cross on your son, the late Pilot Officer C.J. Barton (168669), in recognition of most conspicuous bravery and to enclose a copy of the announcement which will appear in the Royal Air Force Awards Supplement to the London Gazette to be issued on 27th June, 1944.

I am, Sir,
Your obedient Servant,

J.F. Barton Esq.,
171 Elm Road,
New Malden,
Surrey.

Cyril Barton VC

Joyce:

"I remember the day the despatch rider came to our home bringing news of Cyril's Victoria Cross. Dad was home and was so excited but Mum wasn't at all. Dad explained that it was the highest honour that Cyril could have had. Mum said, 'So what, it won't bring him back'. So at that time it didn't mean a thing to Mum. She didn't really want to know.

. . . When I got home from school at lunchtime, I couldn't get near the house because of newspaper reporters. We couldn't get anywhere. They were up the stairs, round the back, in the garden . . . all over the house, pestering my mother with questions and taking photographs, just to make a story . . .

Some time later, when the VC award dawned on her and she realised what it was all about, she was obviously very proud of Cyril and she used to carry it in her handbag everywhere up to the day she died."[4]

[Transcript of letter from Mrs. Barton to the Richardson family]

171 Elm Road
New Malden
Surrey
1/5/45

"Dear Mr. & Mrs. Richardson,
I was very pleased to hear from you. So sorry

not to have answered your letter before now, but really so many people wrote to me, about 600 in all, that I felt so overwhelmed I didn't know how to start answering them. In the end I just got a letter printed and just put a message on each one. Some people had their only son missing, some had boys killed, very much the same as Cyril was, in a crash landing. It was really heartaching to read some of them.

This has been a dreadful war and about time it was over. We all feel war weary don't we? I sincerely hope by now, you have fully recovered from the shock which must have been dreadful at the time. My dear boy would have been so vexed to know he caused any injury to anyone. He was a lovely boy, adored and loved by all who knew him. I was sorry not to have met you while I was at Ryhope but travelling was dreadful at that time and the journey took us twice as long, and the very thought of the crash made my husband ill. He couldn't face it. I wished afterwards that my son and I had come alone, but I hope one day to come again and I will be sure to come and see you. We are all so thankful in this part of the country the V-Bombs have stopped. We had 22 flying bombs on New Malden, eleven people were killed and over 30, 000 houses damaged. My house was damaged; I had windows, doors and walls blown out. We were all praised by our wardens for taking cover when the imminent danger signal was given. We had one rocket about two miles away. They are dreadful things, damage and casualties were very great. This was at Kingston. I thought it would have shook our house down.

My husband and I went to Buckingham Palace on the 5th of December to receive Cyril's VC from the King, who was very kind and sympathetic to us. We have beautiful memories of our dear boy.

My love to you and yours very sincerely,

E. Barton"

Epilogue

"You could sum Cyril up as being a good, solid all-rounder. He was happy. He had great thoughts for his religion and great respect for other people. He was a sportsman . . . had an enormous sense of humour and he was really capable at virtually everything he did."

Joyce Voysey and Cynthia Maidment

"Cyril's life was a short one, but it was a full one. Life is richer for me and for many for having known him. God helping us we shall see that he did not die in vain."

Frank Colquhoun

References

[1] *Interview with Cynthia Maidment and Joyce Voysey, 27th November, 1993*
[2] *Frank Colquhoun 'The Air Pilot's decision', p.22*
[3] *Interview with Cynthia Maidment and Joyce Voysey, 27th November, 1993*
[4] *Ibid.*

Appendix I

Memorial Campaign

Cyril Joe Barton died at Ryhope Colliery on 31st March, 1944, after enduring almost eight hours of hell, when he and his crew took part in the raid on Nuremberg, one of the bloodiest air-battles of World War II. Ninety-six aircraft were shot down or crashed, and another twelve destroyed on the return journeys. A disaster for Bomber Command.

Yet, for forty years or so, no recognition was to be found anywhere in Ryhope, or indeed the North East, of a young man who had gallantly sacrificed everything in bringing his crippled Halifax back to England, against almost impossible odds. At the end of this terrible ordeal, he managed to steer the falling bomber away from what could have been a terrible tragedy. Apart from the end house of West Terrace, he avoided the homes below him, and the people who occupied them. His three crewmen survived, but he died before receiving hospital treatment. For his actions from beginning to end, he was awarded this country's highest award for gallantry, the Victoria Cross.

Having witnessed the last moments from my bedroom window, the memory of that morning fifty years ago has remained with me ever since.

And so it was, when, some five and a half years later, I was called into the RAF myself on National Service. Following the training, I was posted to RAF Leeming, in North Yorkshire. This was when I made my first enquiries about Cyril Barton VC. I learned that Canadian squadrons of No. 6 Group had operated from Leeming with the Halifax Mk II and III, and so wondered if it were possible for him to have flown from there. It was some two years or so later I discovered he was with 578 Squadron at Burn, just outside Selby, which was about thirty miles down the road.

When I returned to my civilian work in 1953 as a printer, I would often reflect on the incident in 1944. This, I believe, was probably due to me having gained knowledge and experience of what service life was like in the Royal Air Force, and found out for myself what it must have been like going out on operations. Even though it was after the war, eighteen aircrew were killed on training exercises during my time at Leeming.

For many years, I often wondered why no mention of Cyril Barton was ever to be found in Ryhope. Time and time again I would visit the spot where LK797(E) came to rest. The 'Hope' was my playground as a boy and the ravine below the gangway (footbridge) with its 'Windy Cave' and others, were always curious places to explore. The rear fuselage and broken tail unit of the Halifax bomber, at an angle of almost upright, stood like a monument of its own for some five weeks or so. Certainly it seemed like ages before it was brought down from the hill when salvage work commenced in the colliery yard. I was there the Saturday morning the 'Queen Mary' arrived (long, extra-long trailer used by RAF for transportation of aircraft parts) and photographs were taken of the rear fuselage by an RAF photographer.

Often, I would delve into the crash, making an inquiry here and there, writing to various magazines for information, and in particular of the crewmen. I eventually contacted the squadron, and in the early 1980's was adopted by them when they discovered how I had been involved in my research and efforts for the recognition of Cyril Barton VC.

I first met gunners, Fred Brice and Harry Wood, in Birmingham in 1983, along with navigator Len Lambert, when the painting 'For Valour' was given its press release. Later, I met Wally Crate, the Canadian bomb-aimer at the 40th squadron reunion in 1984. Maurice Trousdale, the flight engineer, died on 31st December, 1976.

MONDAY, APRIL 22, 1985. No. 35,243 (112th Year). 14p

We must remember this hero

TODAY the Echo joins Wearsider Alan Mitcheson in his fight to get a memorial to wartime V.C. Pilot Officer Cyril Barton at Ryhope.

Forty-one years ago Barton steered his crashing Halifax bomber away from houses at Ryhope and was killed. He undoubtedly saved many lives in doing so.

Three weeks ago we expressed our dismay that Sunderland Planning Department did not want to

PAGE ONE COMMENT

recognise Barton's heroism because he had no other connection with the area.

Mr Mitcheson wants a simple plaque set in stone somewhere in Ryhope to commemorate this brave deed. We and lots of our readers agree with him and we are prepared to fund the memorial if the

Planning Authority will provide a suitable site. Ryhope Green would be a suitable place.

We believe Sunderland is big enough to mark this young man's heroism. In 1944 the nation thought enough of him to award him the Victoria Cross. We are very late in doing anything, but are we to use that as an excuse to say we owe him nothing at all? Let us be honest and recognise our debt to a brave young man. We repeat our appeal to the Planning Department to think again.

Echo, Sunderland, Saturday, April 27, 1985—5

Any views? drop a line to the editor

Ambulanceman recalls crash

Get cracking Ryhope

AFTER reading about the lack of a memorial to Pilot Officer Barton, V.C., I am left wondering if it is lack of money that is keeping Ryhope from getting one.

If so, why don't they try what we did in Ryhope when we wanted a war memorial after 1914-18.

I remember as a child of five marching from the village school to the villge green, clutching a handfull of pennies to make a mile of pennies around the green.

My father's name is on that memorial, also on the one at Silksworth. So, if there is a fund, I will send my widow's mite. Get cracking, Ryhope.

(Mrs) D. Dobinson
Cottages Road,
Seaburn.

I HAVE been following with great interest the efforts of Alan Mitcheson to have a memorial to Pilot Officer Cyril Barton, V.C., at Ryhope.

As a boy he remembers quite well what a tragedy there could have been if it had not been for the unselfish action of this young airman, who steered his crippled bomber clear of the houses which were directly below him before crashing.

Let no one forget also what this courageous young man had endured beforehand when he was over Germany.

I was the ambulance driver at the colliery who took the young pilot and three crew to hospital. Barton died before receiving attention.

I am 89 now, have lived in Ryhope all my life, and was shocked, absolutely disgusted, and thoroughly ashamed to learn that Sunderland Council had

This is your page. If you have any views write to: The Editor, Echo, Pennywell Industrial Estate, Sunderland SR4 9ER.

rejected this recognition because he didn't belong here. They should think again about this.

Harry Hicks
Ryemount Road,
Ryhope.

Disgraceful

I AM sure every ex-service person will welcome your front page Comment (Echo, April 22), in the fight for Alan Mitcheson's tribute to Pilot Officer Cyril Barton, V.C.

Some day, the person or persons, within our Civic Centre must be named, so that when they come round begging for our votes as councillors, they can be told where to go, how to get there and what to do when they arrive.

The disgraceful decision they made regarding a memorial to this very gallant and brave man must be reversed and we are all of the same mind.

A Chape
(Chairman Sunderland Companion Club)
Merrington Court,
Sunderland

Organize appeal

AFTER reading so many letters in support of Alan Mitcheson's efforts to have a memorial erected to Pilot Officer Cyril Barton, V.C., I feel I must offer my support.

Being chairman of Ryhope Workmen's Club, I am in a position to invite Alan, and anyone else who shares the same views, to form a committee and appeal to the people in the Civic Centre who actually turned down this memorial.

If it was turned down for financial reasons organize an appeal to the public. Incidentally, I actually entered the aircraft after the crash to try and help, but was immediately told to get out as it was likely to explode. Perhaps I might be able to help now.

Thomas Crake
Bevan Avenue,
Ryhope.

Fred Brice and Harry Wood died within three month of each other in 1990. Jack Kay, the wireless operator lives in Sussex, Len Lambert in Ponteland. Wally Crate lives in Ontario.

When it became known that the old colliery site at Ryhope was to be converted into a golf course and parkland, I started making approaches to Sunderland Council with a suggestion that they name the eventual site after Cyril Barton VC. As I have already stated, there was no recognition of him anywhere up here; down South where he belonged, yes, but not here; and I became quite dismayed about this. The first reply from the Council was to inform me that if and when such naming were possible, my suggestion would be given due consideration.

A long time was spent in discussion and negotiation without any progress being made but eventually the council agreed to place a bronze plaque on Ryhope village green war memorial.

The unveiling was performed on Remembrance Sunday, 10th November 1985 by the sisters of P.O. Barton VC, Mrs Cynthia Maidment and Mrs Joyce Voysey.

At the time of my campaign being shelved, I tried other avenues of recognition. I contacted the Borough Engineer to see if it were possible to have a road or suchlike named after Cyril Barton and shortly afterwards a small, private housing complex on the site of the former Poplars club was named 'Halifax Place', dedicated to the crew and aircraft. Arrangements for the unveiling were left in my hands, and so I invited Len Lambert (Navigator) down from Ponteland to carry out the unveiling ceremony of the street sign. That was in April 1986.

At the time of the opening of Ryhope Golf Club, the Council approached the Barton family

Success at last – Left to right: Alan Mitcheson, Joyce Voysey and Cynthia Maidment after the unveiling of the bronze plaque, Ryhope War Memorial.

with the suggestion that Cyril Barton's place in Ryhope's history should be recognised. The family chose to name a room used by young people 'The Barton Room'. The ceremony was attended by Cyril Barton's sisters who subsequently donated two trophies to the Golf Club.

On the same occasion a plaque commemorating the deaths of mine workers at Ryhope Colliery was unveiled thus uniting in recognition the mining community with Cyril Barton.

Achieving proper recognition for Cyril Barton has been a lengthy process involving protracted and not always successful negotiation with all of the parties involved.

However, I am very pleased to say that today, the City Council has made possible the production of a brief but nevertheless first-class account of this young man's life, for which I personally am exceedingly grateful.

Alan Mitcheson

Left to right: Alwyn Carr (Bomber Command Association), Alan Mitcheson and Len Lambert

Gunner remembers

AS one of the surviving members of Pilot Officer Barton's crew, who attended the service and unveiling of the memorial plaque at the Ryhope War Memorial, may I say thank you to the people of Ryhope for their unforgettable welcome.

For me to have reason to return after 41 years, to meet people who helped us on that fateful morning, people like Mr Lawther who pulled us out of the wreckage, Harry Hicks the ambulance driver, Sister Herbert, Sister Sparkes who were then at Cherry Knowle Hospital, just to be able to say a humble thank-you and shake their hand, is something I will never forget.

Another touching moment for me, was after the unveiling ceremony when I was approached by an elderly gentleman, who asked if I was a member of Cyril Barton's crew or in anyway connected, when I said I was, he took from his pocket a copy of last Friday's Echo containing the article headed "Wartime Memories of flying hero linger on". He had brought it along hoping to meet someone, who would like it to keep as a memento, I was very pleased to accept it.

The reception at the Community Centre, where we were well and truly refreshed, is another thing I will remember. The number of people who came to shake hands, say hello pleased to meet you, was overwhelming. My thanks also to the people who looked after our welfare there.

At the end of the day, my thanks must go to Mr Alan Mitchison, who after a long campaign eventually reached his goal, the burning ambition of the 12-year-old lad who saw us crash. Once again my thanks to friends in Ryhope.

Freddie Brice
(Rear gunner)
Clevedon,
Avon.

GALLANT MAN HONOURED

I WAS very proud to be present at Ryhope last Sunday and to see so many present in St Paul's Church; also at the War Memorial when my pilot, Cyril Joe Barton, V.C., was honoured by the community. I know he too would have been delighted.

It must have been of immense satisfaction for Alan Mitcheson, who campaigned so long and so vigorously, to see all his efforts come to a head.

In addition what happiness there was for me in meeting once more two of the gentlemen who helped us all those many years ago. First, I met Harry Hicks who drove the ambulance that took us to the emergency ward at Ryhope Hospital, and later Mr Les Lawther, who managed to extricate the three of us from the fuselage of our wrecked Halifax bomber. There were Maurice Trousdale, the flight engineer, Fred Brice, the rear gunner, and the writer who was the mid-upper gunner.

We also met Eva Sparks, night sister, and Celia Herbert, day sister at Ryhope Hospital. What memories these ladies brought back to me of the period spent in the emergency ward prior to being fit enough to be transferred to the R.A.F. hospital in Northallerton.

One person I did not meet, and one I would very much like to have seen again, was the chap in the first aid room at Ryhope Colliery who gave me the most delicious cup of hot, sweet tea that I have ever tasted.

I want to congratulate the ladies and the gentlemen at the Community Centre for providing the excellent meal which followed the service at the War Memorial, it really was appreciated.

May I end by expressing my gratitude to your readers who wrote backing Alan Mitcheson's campaign to have a memorial erected in Ryhope, where Cy Barton died so tragically in 1944. He was one of the most gallant men it has been my privilege to fly and serve with.

H. D. Wood
Allesley Village
Coventry

Letters to the Sunderland Echo following the unveiling of the Cyril Barton plaque, November 1985

Worth every mile

MY WIFE and I were among the many people invited to St Paul's Church Ryhope on Sunday, November 10, for the Remembrance Service and the dedication of a plaque to our friend, Pilot Officer Cyril Barton, V.C.

We found the service most moving and memorable, not the least because of the music and the sincere way in which the packed congregation joined in. We were truly overwhelmed by the wonderful support which the good people of Ryhope gave

We had motored some 700 miles to attend this ceremony and it was worth every mile which we had to travel. May we therefore thank everybody concerned for this memorable day. We thank the Echo and the citizens of Ryhope for the support given to Alan Mitcheson who has campaigned so tirelessly over many years for this memorial to our dear friend. We thank all the organisations which paraded so proudly to honour our dead. Thank you to the officials who planned the event and made it possible and finally a big thank-you to the Ryhope Community Centre for their very welcome hospitality after the service.

Cyril and his young crew were very special people, the best this country had. Ryhope has demonstrated that their sacrifice was not unnoticed, or forgotten. God bless you all.

Maurice Divey
Kingston Vale,
London.

Ryhope 1985 – grand reunion. Left to right: Les Lawther, rescuer; Harry Hicks, ambulance driver; Maurice Divey, friend of Cyril Barton

Ryhope 1985. Left to right: Len Lambert, Freddie Brice, H.D. 'Timber' Wood

Appendix II

P/O Cyril Barton VC Memorial List

No.	Item	Description
1.	Engraved copper Ewer	Parish of Elvedon. Used for baptismal water. Barton's birthplace 5th June 1921.
2.	Portrait in oils	Presented to the Barton family by Handley Page Ltd.
3.	Photograph	In the VCs' gallery, RAF Cranwell.
4.	Portrait and Citation	In Malden council chambers. Later transferred to New Malden Library staircase on merger with Kingston.
5.	Barton Green & Pavilion	Road and Pavilion in New Malden named after Barton. Bronze plaque on pavilion wall. Used by theatre group.
6.	Photograph	In 1st Oxshot Scout HQ, Surrey. He was in the scout group.
7.	Tree	Planted in the grounds of Beverley School, New Malden.
8.	Plaque	In Beverley School Barton Library and Resource Centre. Named after Barton who attended this school.
9.	Plaque	A Barrack block at RAF Station, Hemswell, near. Gainsborough, Lincolnshire. Named after Barton.
10.	Housing complex	Halifax Place, Ryhope. Named after Barton's aircraft.
11.	Plaque and Citation	At Cherry Knowle Hospital, Ryhope. Barton and crew were taken here after the crash in colliery grounds.
12.	Plaque	Commemorating the re-organisation of the Sunderland & Ryhope hospitals into the Barton Memorial Unit.
13.	Plaque	A large bronze plaque attached to the Ryhope war memorial in a civic ceremony on Remembrance Sunday, 1985.
14.	Headstone	Raised by the War Graves Commission in Kingston Cemetery, Barton's last resting place.
15.	Portrait and Citation	In the HQ of 4th Malden Air Scouts.
16.	Photograph and Citation	Shown in a display case at RAF Museum, Hendon, London.
17.	General Plaque	Parnell's Ltd of Yate put up a commemorative plaque to all their employees. Barton worked in their DO at Tolworth, Surrey.

18.	General Plaque	The English-Speaking Union of Atlanta, USA placed a plaque to all the RAF boys who trained in St. Clement Dane's Church, London. Barton is especially mentioned.
19.	Plaque	Road named after Barton on the airfield at Elvington, where the Yorkshire Air Museum is located.
20.	Painting	A painting by K.B. Hancock showing Barton's 'plane being attacked by German fighters. Its title was 'For Valour. Cy. Barton VC'. Prints were sold at £15 each and proceeds went to RAF Bomber Command Museum and the RAF Benevolent Fund. It was launched on Wednesday, 28th September, 1983.
21.	Music	The Barton Memorial March, by Roy Horabin. Played for its first public performance in October 1992 by the Newcastle City Temple Silver Band of the Salvation Army.
22.	Plaque	The Barton Room in the club house at Ryhope Golf Course.
23.	Trophies	Two silver cups for golf competitions at Ryhope Golf Club.

Unveiling of the memorial plaque at Cherry Knowle Hospital, January 1991, by Cyril Barton's sisters (L–R) Cynthia, Pam and Joyce

Appendix III

'Victor'

Bibliography

I Manuscript Collections

Department of Research and Information Services, RAF Museum, Hendon, London:
Documents relating to Cyril Barton
ASO Summary of the Nuremberg Raid 1, April, 1944
Certificates of Qualification as First Pilot
Flight log
Operational Crew List, 30th March, 1944
Recommendations for Honours and Awards

Alan Mitcheson collection

Mrs. Joyce Voysey:
Copy of letter from F. Brice to Sgt. Bowyer, dated 1st December, 1968
Cyril Barton's Diary
Letters written by Cyril Barton to members of his family
Mr. Barton's letter to Cyril regarding his decision to join the RAF
The 'Crew Line Book'
Photographs of Cyril Barton, family and friends
'The Air Pilot's Decision', F. Colquhoun
School reports

Letters in possession of W.W. Lowther from:
Enid Barnet, Fred Carr, Maurice Divey, C.P. Lamb, Cynthia Maidment, Alan Mitcheson, Joyce Voysey and Mary Wilkinson.

Transcripts of taped interviews in possession of W.W. Lowther:
Len Lambert, Les Lawther, Arthur Milburn, Joyce Voysey and Cynthia Maidment, Ken and Tom Richardson.

II Newspapers

London Gazette
Sunderland Echo and Shipping Gazette

III Secondary Books

Bowyer C. 'For Valour'   (Harper Collins, 1978)
Jones G.   'Raider'   (Harper Collins, 1978)
Middlebrook M. 'The Nuremberg Raid, 30-31 March 1944'   (Penguin, 1973)